"This series is a tremendous resource f(understanding of how the gospel is w pastors and scholars doing gospel business from all the Scriptures. This is a biblical and theo- logical feast preparing God's people to apply the entire Bible to all of life with heart and mind wholly committed to Christ's priorities."

BRYAN CHAPELL, President Emeritus, Covenant Theological Seminary; Senior Pastor, Grace Presbyterian Church, Peoria, Illinois

"Mark Twain may have smiled when he wrote to a friend, 'I didn't have time to write you a short letter, so I wrote you a long letter.' But the truth of Twain's remark remains serious and universal, because well-reasoned, compact writing requires extra time and extra hard work. And this is what we have in the Crossway Bible study series *Knowing the Bible*. The skilled au- thors and notable editors provide the contours of each book of the Bible as well as the grand theological themes that bind them together as one Book. Here, in a 12-week format, are care- fully wrought studies that will ignite the mind and the heart."

R. KENT HUGHES, Visiting Professor of Practical Theology, Westminster Theological Seminary

"*Knowing the Bible* brings together a gifted team of Bible teachers to produce a high-quality series of study guides. The coordinated focus of these materials is unique: biblical content, provocative questions, systematic theology, practical application, and the gospel story of God's grace presented all the way through Scripture."

PHILIP G. RYKEN, President, Wheaton College

"These *Knowing the Bible* volumes provide a significant and very welcome variation on the general run of inductive Bible studies. This series provides substantial instruction, as well as teaching through the very questions that are asked. *Knowing the Bible* then goes even further by showing how any given text links with the gospel, the whole Bible, and the formation of theology. I heartily endorse this orientation of individual books to the whole Bible and the gospel, and I applaud the demonstration that sound theology was not something invented later by Christians, but is right there in the pages of Scripture."

GRAEME L. GOLDSWORTHY, former lecturer, Moore Theological College; author, *According to Plan*, *Gospel and Kingdom*, *The Gospel in Revelation*, and *Gospel and Wisdom*

"What a gift to earnest, Bible-loving, Bible-searching believers! The organization and structure of the Bible study format presented through the *Knowing the Bible* series is so well conceived. Students of the Word are led to understand the content of passages through perceptive, guided questions, and they are given rich insights and application all along the way in the brief but illuminating sections that conclude each study. What potential growth in depth and breadth of understanding these studies offer! One can only pray that vast numbers of believers will discover more of God and the beauty of his Word through these rich studies."

BRUCE A. WARE, Professor of Christian Theology, The Southern Baptist Theological Seminary

I Kings 138:40 Deut 6:3-4 10:12-14 11:18-3
Ex 25:8-9, 26-30

KNOWING THE BIBLE

J. I. Packer, Theological Editor
Dane C. Ortlund, Series Editor
Lane T. Dennis, Executive Editor

•   •   •   •   •   •   •

Genesis	Psalms	Jonah, Micah, and	Ephesians
Exodus	Proverbs	Nahum	Philippians
Leviticus	Ecclesiastes	Haggai, Zechariah,	Colossians and
Numbers	Song of Solomon	and Malachi	Philemon
Deuteronomy	Isaiah	Matthew	1–2 Thessalonians
Joshua	Jeremiah	Mark	1–2 Timothy and
Judges	Lamentations,	Luke	Titus
Ruth and Esther	Habakkuk, and	John	Hebrews
1–2 Samuel	Zephaniah	Acts	James
1–2 Kings	Ezekiel	Romans	1–2 Peter and Jude
1–2 Chronicles	Daniel	1 Corinthians	1–3 John
Ezra and Nehemiah	Hosea	2 Corinthians	Revelation
Job	Joel, Amos, and	Galatians	
	Obadiah		

•   •   •   •   •   •   •

J. I. PACKER is Board of Governors' Professor of Theology at Regent College (Vancouver, BC). Dr. Packer earned his DPhil at the University of Oxford. He is known and loved worldwide as the author of the best-selling book *Knowing God*, as well as many other titles on theology and the Christian life. He serves as the General Editor of the ESV Bible and as the Theological Editor for the *ESV Study Bible*.

LANE T. DENNIS is President of Crossway, a not-for-profit publishing ministry. Dr. Dennis earned his PhD from Northwestern University. He is Chair of the ESV Bible Translation Oversight Committee and Executive Editor of the *ESV Study Bible*.

DANE C. ORTLUND is Executive Vice President of Bible Publishing and Bible Publisher at Crossway. He is a graduate of Covenant Theological Seminary (MDiv, ThM) and Wheaton College (BA, PhD). Dr. Ortlund has authored several books and scholarly articles in the areas of Bible, theology, and Christian living.

1–2 CHRONICLES

A 12-WEEK STUDY

James Duguid

WHEATON, ILLINOIS

Knowing the Bible: 1–2 Chronicles, A 12-Week Study

Copyright © 2018 by Crossway

Published by Crossway
        1300 Crescent Street
        Wheaton, Illinois 60187

Some content used in this study guide has been adapted from the *ESV Study Bible* (Crossway), copyright 2008 by Crossway, pages 697–798. Used by permission. All rights reserved.

Cover design: Simplicated Studio

First printing 2018

Printed in the United States of America

Trade paperback ISBN: 978-1-4335-6105-4
ePub ISBN: 978-1-4335-6108-5
PDF ISBN: 978-1-4335-6106-1
Mobipocket ISBN: 978-1-4335-6107-8

Crossway is a publishing ministry of Good News Publishers.

VP			27	26	25	24	23	22	21	20	19	18
15	14	13	12	11	10	9	8	7	6	5	4	3	2	1

TABLE OF CONTENTS

SERIES PREFACE

KNOWING THE BIBLE, as the series title indicates, was created to help readers know and understand the meaning, the message, and the God of the Bible. Each volume in the series consists of 12 units that progressively take the reader through a clear, concise study of one or more books of the Bible. In this way, any given volume can fruitfully be used in a 12-week format either in group study, such as in a church-based context, or in individual study. Of course, these 12 studies could be completed in fewer or more than 12 weeks, as convenient, depending on the context in which they are used.

Each study unit gives an overview of the text at hand before digging into it with a series of questions for reflection or discussion. The unit then concludes by highlighting the gospel of grace in each passage ("Gospel Glimpses"), identifying whole-Bible themes that occur in the passage ("Whole-Bible Connections"), and pinpointing Christian doctrines that are affirmed in the passage ("Theological Soundings").

The final component to each unit is a section for reflecting on personal and practical implications from the passage at hand. The layout provides space for recording responses to the questions proposed, and we think readers need to do this to get the full benefit of the exercise. The series also includes definitions of key words. These definitions are indicated by a note number in the text and are found at the end of each chapter.

Lastly, to help understand the Bible in this deeper way, we urge readers to use the ESV Bible and the *ESV Study Bible*, which are available in various print and digital formats, including online editions at esv.org. The *Knowing the Bible* series is also available online.

May the Lord greatly bless your study as you seek to know him through knowing his Word.

J. I. Packer
Lane T. Dennis

WEEK 1: OVERVIEW

Getting Acquainted

The books of 1–2 Chronicles are a remix. Their anonymous author (we will call him the Chronicler) seeks to provide a different angle on the history recounted in the books of Genesis through 2 Kings, reworking it with new details and a fresh perspective. Sometimes the accounts in 1–2 Chronicles may seem contradictory to those earlier in Scripture, but in fact they are complementary perspectives, bringing out different aspects of the same events.

The Chronicler's original audience consisted of saints toiling for God's kingdom in days of relative obscurity. He wanted them to know that God had made an abiding promise to dwell with his people. He also wanted to challenge them with a picture of what God's ideal people ought to look like. They were to stand with God's chosen king, who ought to embody the virtues of David and Solomon. They were to support the work of the temple, being careful to worship God exactly as he commanded and to rejoice before him in song. Although he does not deny that sin has generational dimensions, the Chronicler wants us to think about the time we have before us and to realize that *now* is the time to obey God. Each generation must make this choice; obedience will lead to blessing, whereas disobedience will lead to the consequences of God's discipline.

God is the main character in this story. He is a God who has chosen Israel, Jerusalem, and the line of David. His grace, his initiative, stands behind every willing human inclination and gift. His compassion and forgiveness are endless to those who turn to him in repentance. The Chronicler wants us to look to God for help, and he assures us of God's plan to bless his people by dwelling with them forever.

Placing 1–2 Chronicles in the Larger Story

First and Second Chronicles are the final books in the original order of the Hebrew Bible and were two of the last books of the Old Testament to be written. In a sense, 1–2 Chronicles embrace and unify the whole Old Testament into one coherent story. The books were first written to people looking back on the history of Israel from the other side of the exile.[1] First and Second Chronicles pointed them back to the past for examples of how to live as a people, looking especially to the ideal models of David and Solomon. The books also provide examples of the danger of sin and its consequences. Most of all, they point God's people to the importance of repentance and reform: turning away from our sin and toward God in order to receive his forgiveness and blessing. The people of Israel were stubborn in their sin. They did not listen to God or his prophets, despite repeated calls to turn back to their God. Although God disciplined them with affliction for their sin, they still did not repent. The Chronicler thus warns his hearers to be quick to repent.

The Chronicler also points his readers toward the future, toward the hope of God's promise. The two cornerstone institutions of the people of Israel, the Davidic monarchy and the temple, are both founded upon God's unbreakable promise. Despite the obstacles in their way, the people can have confidence that God will keep his word to Israel, and this knowledge should give them confidence to engage joyfully in the work of God's kingdom.

Key Verse

"If my people who are called by my name humble themselves, and pray and seek my face and turn from their wicked ways, then I will hear from heaven and will forgive their sin and heal their land." (2 Chron. 7:14)

Date and Historical Background

Chronicles is anonymous and cannot be dated precisely. The best clue in the book is the genealogy of David in 1 Chronicles 3, which is traced down through Zerubbabel to six subsequent generations. Given that Zerubbabel returned to the land after the edict of Cyrus in 539 BC, this would place the book somewhere in the 400s BC, if one allows about a century for his family tree to grow to this extent. This assumes, of course, that the Chronicler has brought the genealogy down to his own day: if not, the book could have been written quite a bit later.

The time from 539 to 331 BC in the ancient Near East is known as the Persian period, as it was dominated by the Persian Empire. The period began favorably, with King Cyrus allowing the Jews to return to Jerusalem and rebuild the temple, but not all of the Persian kings were as hospitable to God's people. Ezra–Nehemiah records the efforts of surrounding nations to thwart the building of the temple and the walls of Jerusalem, and these efforts succeeded in turning the Persian kings against Judah. This period was marked by new beginnings and hope for the future but also by difficulties and setbacks, bringing a constant awareness of Judah's vulnerability to vastly more powerful Gentile overlords.

The effort to rebuild the temple in Jerusalem was ultimately successful. The Chronicler shows a keen interest in the history of the Levites, and he himself may have been a Levite or a priest, connected to the temple in some way. Tradition identifies the Chronicler as Ezra, but there is no evidence in the book itself to prove this claim. It has sometimes been believed that the Chronicler was also the author of Ezra–Nehemiah, but more recent scholarship highlights the differences between these books, suggesting they had different authors.

Outline

I. The People of God: Genealogies of the Tribes of Israel (1 Chronicles 1–9)

    A. The election of Israel (1 Chronicles 1:1–2:2)
    B. Judah, David, and Simeon (1 Chronicles 2:3–4:43)
    C. The Transjordanian tribes (1 Chronicles 5)
    D. Levi (1 Chronicles 6)
    E. The northern tribes (1 Chronicles 7)
    F. The genealogy of Saul (1 Chronicles 8)
    G. The genealogy of the returnees (1 Chronicles 9:1–34)
    H. Second genealogy of Saul (1 Chronicles 9:35–44)

II. God Chooses David and Gives Him the Plan for the Temple (1 Chronicles 10–29)

    A. The rise of David (1 Chronicles 10–12)
    B. David and the ark (1 Chronicles 13–16)
    C. The covenant with David (1 Chronicles 17)
    D. David's wars (1 Chronicles 18–20)
    E. David's census (1 Chronicles 21)
    F. David's first charge (1 Chronicles 22)
    G. David's organization of the temple personnel (1 Chronicles 23–27)
    H. David's second charge (1 Chronicles 28–29)

III. God Chooses Solomon and Helps Him Build the Temple (2 Chronicles 1–9)

    A. Solomon's wealth and wisdom (2 Chronicles 1)
    B. Solomon and Hiram (2 Chronicles 2)
    C. Solomon's construction of the temple (2 Chronicles 3–5)

    D. The temple dedication (2 Chronicles 6–7)

    E. Solomon's wealth and wisdom (2 Chronicles 8–9)

IV. The Kings of Judah: Good, Bad, and Mixed (2 Chronicles 10–36)

    A. Rehoboam (2 Chronicles 10–12)

    B. Abijah (2 Chronicles 13)

    C. Asa (2 Chronicles 14–16)

    D. Jehoshaphat (2 Chronicles 17–20)

    E. Jehoram (2 Chronicles 21)

    F. Ahaziah (2 Chronicles 22)

    G. Joash (2 Chronicles 23–24)

    H. Amaziah (2 Chronicles 25)

    I. Uzziah (2 Chronicles 26)

    J. Jotham (2 Chronicles 27)

    K. Ahaz (2 Chronicles 28)

    L. Hezekiah (2 Chronicles 29–32)

    M. Manasseh and Amon (2 Chronicles 33)

    N. Josiah (2 Chronicles 34–35)

    O. Jehoahaz, Jehoiakim, Jehoiachin, Zedekiah, and the end (2 Chronicles 36)

As You Get Started

If you were to summarize the whole story of Israel's history in a few broad strokes, how would you do so? What would be its most important parts? What do you remember about the stories of David and Solomon? What do you remember about the temple and why it was important?

What is worship, and why is it an important part of the Christian life? Why do we sing songs? What does this tell us about God and about ourselves?

How does God's discipline work? Is suffering always a result of punishment for sin? Does God's forgiveness always remove the consequences of sin? Do you have any questions or confusions about this topic that you wish to explore in the course of this study?

Is the Christian life all about our effort, God's effort, or both? How can God's promises be certain if the obedience of sinners—who are constantly liable to disobey—is also necessary?

Definition

[1] **Exile** – Several relocations of large groups of Israelites/Jews have occurred throughout history, but "the exile" typically refers to the Babylonian exile, that is, Nebuchadnezzar's relocation of residents of the southern kingdom of Judah to Babylon in 586 BC. (Residents of the northern kingdom of Israel had been resettled by Assyria in 722 BC.) After Babylon came under Persian rule, several waves of Jewish exiles returned and repopulated Judah.

Week 2: Family Roots

1 Chronicles 1–9

▲

The Place of the Passage

The Chronicler begins with a genealogy. To his readers, who are learning how to live as a reestablished nation in the Promised Land, he presents a vision for a united Israel. But this vision is not a new invention, and the Chronicler uses genealogies to show that the authority for this vision is rooted in the past: in the division of the land by Moses and Joshua and the organization of worship by David. This vision of Israel as a harmonious family, in which each tribe is given its rightful place, sets the standard for the evaluation of Israel's successes and failures as the rest of Israel's story unfolds throughout the book.

The Big Picture

First Chronicles 1–9 shows us a vision of a united Israel, with Judah in the lead, Benjamin at a place of prominence in the rear, and all centered on the priests and Levites and the worship of God.

Reflection and Discussion

Read through the complete passage for this study, 1 Chronicles 1–9. Then review the questions below concerning this section of 1–2 Chronicles and write your notes on them. (For further background, see the *ESV Study Bible*, pages 705–717; available online at www.esv.org.)

1. The Election of Israel (1:1–2:2)

The Chronicler retells the whole story of Genesis, from Adam to the sons of Jacob, in one chapter. Notice especially the diverging branches: Shem, Ham, and Japheth (1 Chron. 1:4); Isaac and Ishmael (1:28); Esau and Israel (1:34). Which of these branches is elaborated first in each case? The Chronicler passes nation after nation before our eyes, making us wait in suspense for God's chosen people to appear. What does this tell us about God's plan of election?[1]

2. Judah, Simeon, and the Transjordanian Tribes (2:3–5:26)

Consider the stories of Er (2:3) and Achan/Achar (2:7). "Achar" sounds like the word for "troubler" in Hebrew—a pun by the author on Achan's name (see Joshua 7 for more of Achan's story). His inclusion in the genealogy is striking, since he has no famous ancestors and no children; he is included to make a point. What do these stories demonstrate about the consequences of disobeying God?

Compare the genealogy of Caleb in 2:42–50 with his genealogy in Numbers 32:12. Consider also the genealogy of Othniel in 1 Chronicles 4:13 and Judges

1:13. Both of these men are Kenizzites. Who were the Kenizzites (see Gen. 15:18–21)? Notice also in 1 Chronicles 1:51b–54 that Kenaz is a chief of Edom, not Israel. If Kenaz was an Edomite, why are these two Kenizzites included in the tribe of Judah (4:13)?

A big theme in Chronicles is that the sins of previous generations cannot irredeemably curse you if you repent and turn to God. How do the stories of these two Kenizzites demonstrate this point?

The Chronicler begins his genealogy with Judah in first place, and at the center of Judah is the genealogy of David's line of kings in chapter 3. What does this say about the place of David and his descendants in the people of Israel? The line of David is continued after the exile in verses 17–24 for several generations through the line of Zerubbabel. Does this testify to a hope for the future?

Consider the story of Jabez in 4:9–10. Jabez is born under a curse; in fact, his very name sounds like a Hebrew word meaning "pain, hardship." So why is he blessed?

Read Genesis 49:5–7 and compare that passage with 1 Chronicles 4:27. Why do you think Shimei, alone among his brothers, escapes the curse on his tribe? Note that the names Simeon, Mishma, and Shimei all sound like the Hebrew word for "to listen" or "to obey."

As the eastern tribes go to war in 5:18–22, they fight together as a unit, demonstrating the unity the Chronicler is advocating for Israel in his own day. What else contributes to their success (vv. 20, 22)? What leads to their ultimate downfall (vv. 25–26)?

3. Levi and the Northern Tribes (6:1–9:44)

Notice the centrality of the priests and the Levites to the Chronicler's vision of Israel. They are given extensive attention in chapter 6 and then again in 9:10–33. What are the reasons for this centrality (see 6:31, 49, 54)? What does this say about the place of worship among God's people?

The other clans are all given their place, but notice the repeated emphasis on Benjamin, which has three genealogies listed (7:6–12; 8:1–40; and 9:35–44). Why do you think the Chronicler places such emphasis on Benjamin? Consider the story of Saul and David. What might the Chronicler be trying to say about how we should respond to historic divisions among God's people?

Read through the following three sections on *Gospel Glimpses, Whole-Bible Connections*, and *Theological Soundings*. Then take time to consider the *Personal Implications* these sections may have for you.

Gospel Glimpses

THE CURSE UNDONE. The Chronicler places great emphasis on the fact that God punishes sin, as we see with Er and Achan. But at the same time he also emphasizes that sin can be forgiven if a sinner repents and turns to God. The Chronicler is especially concerned to show us that we are not doomed by the sins of the past. Those born under a curse, such as Caleb, Shimei, or Jabez, may receive blessing instead if they repent and turn to God for deliverance. This is good news for all of us who fell in Adam, but especially for those who feel trapped in patterns of sin inherited from their families.

THE PEOPLE OF GOD. The Chronicler begins by showing us God's choice of Israel out of all the nations of the earth. He shows us a vision of God's people living in unity, where each tribe and family and clan and person has a place in which to dwell and a role to play. We might have thought that this vision was scrapped when God's people rejected him and he sent them into exile. Yet God is still determined to fulfill his plan for Israel. His purposes to create a holy people for himself have not been defeated by human sin, and they abide for the Chronicler's generation—and for ours.

Whole-Bible Connections

THE INCLUSION OF THE GENTILES. Many Gentiles appear in these chapters, including Judah's Bath-shua (2:3), Jarha (2:34), Caleb (2:42), David's Bath-shua (3:5), Othniel (4:13), and Bithiah (4:17). God's blessing for Abraham was for the peoples of the earth to be blessed through him (Gen. 12:3), and those Gentiles who are willing to join themselves to Israel and Israel's God are included in that blessing. The prophets look forward to a day in which all of the nations will come to worship Israel's God (Isa. 2:2; 56:6–8), and Paul sees this as beginning to be fulfilled as the gospel bears fruit among the Gentiles (Rom. 15:8–13).

JESUS AS ISRAEL. It is tempting to jump right to a connection with Jesus when reading the hope for a Davidic king found in the forefront of the Chronicler's picture of Israel. This would not be incorrect, but the whole truth is bigger than that: Matthew 2:15 applies to Jesus a prophecy from Hosea 11:1: "Out of Egypt I called my son." This implies that Jesus himself is, in a sense, all of Israel, the fulfillment of the Chronicler's hope for the nation. He is not only the Davidic king but also the Great High Priest (Hebrews 7). God's people, Jew and Gentile, are now united by the one Spirit through the one Lord to the one God (Eph. 4:4–5).

Theological Soundings

ORIGINAL AND HEREDITARY SIN. Sin in the Old Testament is not just an individual issue. Ultimately, we are born sinners because we were represented in the garden by Adam, our covenant head; when *he* sinned, *we* sinned. We call this "original sin." It is also true that sin tends to be passed down from generation to generation. Thus we also find ourselves caught in the specific sins of our immediate histories, families, and communities. But 1–2 Chronicles, together with Ezekiel 18, insists that this is never an excuse for our sin. Inherited sin does not have the final say over our lives—God does. And all those who repent and turn to God may be freed from their inherited sin.

THE CENTRALITY OF WORSHIP. The Chronicler shares the same vision as that found in the book of Revelation: the people of God triumphing through worship (Rev. 5:8–14). The assembly of God's people, gathered for prayer, song, preaching, and the sacraments is the epicenter of God's powerful re-creation of the world. It can be tempting for us to get distracted by other priorities or programs that seem more practical—especially since worship can be such a divisive topic. But Scripture insists that we keep worship at the center, even if that means we have to debate with other Christians (lovingly and charitably!) about how to get it right. For the Chronicler, getting worship right is the key to God's people dwelling in unity.

Personal Implications

Take time to reflect on the implications of 1 Chronicles 1–9 for your own life today. Consider what you have learned that might lead you to praise God, repent of sin, and trust more deeply in his gracious promises. Write down your reflections under the three headings we have considered and on the passage as a whole.

1. Gospel Glimpses

2. Whole-Bible Connections

3. Theological Soundings

4. 1 Chronicles 1–9

As You Finish This Unit . . .

Take a moment now to ask for the Lord's blessing and help as you continue in this study of 1–2 Chronicles. And take a moment also to look back through this unit of study, to reflect on some key things that the Lord may be teaching you.

Definition

[1] **Election** – In theology, God's sovereign choice of people for redemption and eternal life. Also referred to as "predestination."

WEEK 3: DAVID AND THE ARK

1 Chronicles 10–16

The Place of the Passage

Having set out a panoramic view of all Israel through the use of various genealogies, the Chronicler turns to the rise of David. David is the king God chose to deliver his people and establish right worship, and thus his kingship is foundational to the Chronicler's vision of a united people living in the land, centered on the worship of God. Chapters 10–12 highlight the choices made by members of every tribe to throw in their lot with David and join in what God is doing. Chapters 13–16 chronicle the installation of the ark[1] in Jerusalem, one of the first precursors of the construction of the temple. These chapters highlight the danger of improper worship of God and the blessing that true worship brings.

The Big Picture

First Chronicles 10–16 shows us how God restores his people from disaster to blessing by raising up David as a faithful king, who puts the worship of God at the center of national life by installing the ark in Jerusalem.

Reflection and Discussion

Read through the complete passage for this study, 1 Chronicles 10–16. Then review the questions below concerning this section of 1–2 Chronicles and write your notes on them. (For further background, see the *ESV Study Bible*, pages 717–727; available online at www.esv.org.)

1. The Rise of David (10:1–12:40)

Consider 1 Chronicles 10:13–14 and 11:1–3. Why is Saul a bad king? What are the consequences for Israel of Saul's ungodly leadership (see 10:7)? How is David different from Saul? What does this say about what godly leadership should look like?

Chapters 11–12 list people from every tribe of Israel who come to help David during this early period when his kingship is still weak. "Help" is a key word of chapter 12 especially (see vv. 1, 17, 18, 19, 21, and 33). Why does the Chronicler put such emphasis on all of these individual choices to participate in what God is doing?

First Chronicles 12:16–18 emphasizes that David is supported by both Judah and Benjamin, even though Benjamin was the tribe to which Saul belonged. Consider Amasai's Spirit-inspired utterance in 12:18. How does God's help fit together with the need for human helpers? Which side of this divine-human equation is more foundational? What are the benefits of throwing in our lot with God's ordained servant?

2. The Ark (13:1–16:43)

Chapter 13 shows that even David is capable of sinning. Despite all of the good elements that are present in 13:1–4, why does this trip turn to tragedy? Are unity and zeal all that are needed to please God? What else is required?

The Hebrew word *prz*, "bursting out," is a theme word for this section, appearing in place-names such as Perez-uzza and Baal-perazim (13:5–14; 14:8–12). How are the two incidents of God's wrath bursting out (in chapters 13–14) similar and/or different? How can God's "bursting out" be a source of curse but also of blessing?

By the beginning of chapter 15, David is prepared to attempt again to bring the ark up to Jerusalem. What did David learn about God (in chapter 14) that encourages him to try again?

Consider 14:10, 14. Why, ultimately, is David's war against the Philistines successful? How is this different from David's first attempt to move the ark, in the previous chapter?

Read the psalm found in 16:8–36, which combines selections from Psalms 96, 105, and 106 and thus serves as a mini-summary of Book Four of the Psalter. Notice especially 1 Chronicles 16:31. How does God's kingship over the universe fit together with human kingship? Why does the Chronicler's audience need to know that God is the King of the whole world, and not just of Israel?

Consider 16:19–22, 35, which emphasizes God's care for his people and his deliverance of them from the nations. How might these verses have spoken to people in David's day? How might they have spoken to people in the Chronicler's time? What about today?

Read through the following three sections on *Gospel Glimpses*, *Whole-Bible Connections*, and *Theological Soundings*. Then take time to consider the *Personal Implications* these sections may have for you.

▶ Gospel Glimpses

A NEW HOPE. The death of Saul and his sons is a disaster for Israel and serves as an illustration of the consequences of failing to seek to obey God diligently. But it is not the end. Even though Israel has sinned and has been judged, God has not given up on them but is preparing to bless his people again through David. Even Saul's Benjaminite kinsmen, who had supported Saul, can repent and experience God's blessing (1 Chron. 12:29). This would be a message of hope to the Chronicler's original audience as well, as they emerged from the curse of exile.

WRATH AND GRACE. The episode at Perez-uzza (13:5–14) reminds us that our God is a fearsome God who is not to be taken lightly. But the passages that follow show us that God's wrath is not the final word for David, even though he has sinned. Instead, God's fearsome power is arrayed to protect him against his enemies. For those who trust God, even his wrath is a means to bring ultimate blessing in their lives. God's determination to bless cannot be stopped by human sin. For those who turn to God and repent of their sin, he is quick to forgive and to bring blessing out of their curse.

▶ Whole-Bible Connections

THE ELECTION OF JERUSALEM. David's capture of Jerusalem and installation of the ark is a pivotal moment in the history of Israel, beginning the fulfillment of the promise in Deuteronomy that the Lord would choose a place in which to make his name dwell (Deut. 26:1–2). The establishment of a permanent dwelling place for God's name represents the permanence of his commitment to his people, and the promise of Jerusalem echoes in the visions of the prophets (e.g., Ezek. 48:35) and in the New Testament image of God's kingdom as a heavenly Jerusalem (Heb. 12:22–24). The election of the earthly Jerusalem is a picture of God's commitment to establish a permanent dwelling with humans in the new heavens and the new earth.

JESUS, SON OF DAVID. David, as God's chosen king, delivers Israel from her oppressors and brings her back toward obedience to God. But as we see in this chapter, not even David does this perfectly. We are still left waiting for the greater Son of David. The New Testament shows us Jesus as David's heir and thus God's chosen king. In the Gospels, Jesus' kingship is especially connected with deliverance from demonic power: Jesus brings the kingdom of God by delivering his people from their enslavement to the powers of this world and thus freeing them to serve as obedient subjects of God's kingdom (see Matt. 12:22–32).

Theological Soundings

PARTICIPATION IN GOD'S WORK. The parallel between human and divine help in Chronicles invites us to consider how the working of God and humans is related. As Christians, we are indwelt by the Holy Spirit and so are united to God in his working. Paul exemplifies this in Colossians 1:29, where he says that he struggles with the energy that God works within him. On the one hand, the church grows only by the working of each individual part (Eph. 4:16). On the other hand, this is not an equal partnership, for God's work precedes and stands behind all human working (Eph. 2:10). It is through the sovereign power of his Spirit that God raises up his people to serve both the church and the world.

DIVINE AND HUMAN KINGSHIP. As we read about Saul's downfall and David's successes and failures, the Chronicler is teaching us about what human kingship ought to look like. Yet there is more than one king present; in the psalm sung at the installation of the ark, the Levites proclaim, "The LORD reigns!" (1 Chron. 16:31). When human kings fail, God remains his people's perfect King. The problem of a human king who fails to live up to his heavenly model is ultimately solved in Christ, the God-man who perfectly unites divine and human kingship in one person. Through union with him, we are brought into God's kingdom.

Personal Implications

Take time to reflect on the implications of 1 Chronicles 10–16 for your own life today. Consider what you have learned that might lead you to praise God, repent of sin, and trust more deeply in his gracious promises. Write down your reflections under the three headings we have considered and on the passage as a whole.

1. Gospel Glimpses

2. Whole-Bible Connections

3. Theological Soundings

4. 1 Chronicles 10–16

> ### As You Finish This Unit . . .

Take a moment now to ask for the Lord's blessing and help as you continue in this study of 1–2 Chronicles. And take a moment also to look back through this unit of study, to reflect on some key things that the Lord may be teaching you.

Definition

[1] **The ark** – A box of acacia wood overlaid with gold, with rings on each side into which poles were inserted for carrying, with two gold cherubim placed on the top (Ex. 25:10–22). The ark contained a copy of the Ten Commandments and symbolized the footstool of God's throne, and thus his royal presence with his people.

WEEK 4: DAVID AND THE TEMPLE

1 Chronicles 17–22

▲

Now that David's reign is established and the ark has been brought to Jerusalem, the Chronicler begins to describe the building of the temple. God's promise to David in chapter 17 identifies Solomon as the one who will build the temple, and chapters 18–20 describe how God gives his people rest through David's victory in battle and also provides resources for the temple. The story of David's census in chapter 21 describes David's sin and God's mercy and, most importantly, narrates how the location for the temple is divinely identified at the threshing floor of Ornan. Chapter 22 records David's charge to Solomon and the leaders of Israel to build the temple as he passes on this commission to his son in accordance with God's promise. All of these narratives in one way or another prepare the way for the building of the temple.

The Big Picture

First Chronicles 17–22 describes how God both promises to dwell with his people in Solomon's temple and also begins to fulfill this promise by giving Israel rest from her enemies.

> ## Reflection and Discussion

Read through the complete passage for this study, 1 Chronicles 17–22. Then review the questions below concerning this section of 1–2 Chronicles and write your notes on them. (For further background, see the *ESV Study Bible*, pages 728–734; available online at www.esv.org.)

1. The Covenant with David (17:1–27)

David and Nathan both seem to believe that going ahead with the building of the temple is the proper next step, but God disagrees. This is similar to the first attempt to move the ark: something that seems like a great idea to God's people may not actually be part of God's plan. Why does God forbid the construction of the temple at this time (see especially vv. 4–10)? Why is it important that God is going to build a house for David and not vice versa?

What is the difference between the tabernacle and a temple? How might a temple lead us to misunderstand who God is (consider Jer. 7:1–11)? In light of David's prayer in 1 Chronicles 17:16–27, how has God's rejection of David's temple-building plan helped David better to understand who God is?

Compare verses 13–14 with 2 Samuel 7:14–16. What changes do you notice? How has the Chronicler shifted the emphasis of the passage by making these changes?

According to the Chronicler, to whom does the kingdom of Israel ultimately belong? What does it mean for the king to be a son to God? How is this different from God's relationship to Saul?

----

2. David's Wars (18:1–20:8)

In these chapters, the Chronicler takes material from 2 Samuel 8–12 and 2 Samuel 21 and groups it together. He passes over material such as the story of David and Bathsheba to focus on a panoramic view of the military victories God gives to David. What is he trying to emphasize? How do these chapters connect to God's promise in 1 Chronicles 17:9–10?

Chapter 19 focuses on the decision about whether to support David, this time from the point of view of a foolish young king who chooses to disrespect and attack David. In 19:12–13, Joab and Abishai commit to help each other, but according to Joab, who ultimately decides the battle?

On the other hand, the Syrians choose to help the Ammonites (see v. 19). What is the result? How is this a picture of the choice that faces the people of Israel in the Chronicler's day? What about the choice facing the surrounding nations? Consider the story of another Ammonite in Nehemiah 4:1–3.

Consider the following passages: 1 Chronicles 18:7–11; 20:2–3. What do these texts say about the source of the funds for building the temple? Who is it that makes the temple construction possible? How is the Chronicler striking a balance between human effort and divine agency?

3. David's Census and David's Charge (21:1–22:19)

Why is it sinful for David to take a census? Consider Joab's response in 21:3. Here the Chronicler shows us a second example of David's failures. Yet David also repents. What does 21:13–14 tell us about how God responds to repentance?

Although God has compassion on his people, why is sacrifice still necessary to avert the threat completely (21:26–27; see Heb. 9:22)?

Read 1 Chronicles 21:18–22:1. What does this story say about God's ability to bring good even out of his people's sin?

Based on 22:8–9, what is it about Solomon that makes him the right man to build the temple? In what ways does a temple provide more appropriate imagery for a time of rest than would a tabernacle?

According to verses 12–13, what is necessary for Solomon's success? Why is God's gift of wisdom necessary for obeying the law? Why is courage necessary for obeying the law? How are these virtues of wisdom and courage necessary for obeying God in your current context?

Read through the following three sections on *Gospel Glimpses*, *Whole-Bible Connections*, and *Theological Soundings*. Then take time to consider the *Personal Implications* these sections may have for you.

Gospel Glimpses

GOD BUILDS THE HOUSE. Zeal to exalt God's name is a good thing, but sometimes it can lead to a self-centered and proud focus on our own accomplishments. In this passage, God reminds us that our work for God is not the main thing—his work for *us* is. God is not dependent on us; he will sovereignly accomplish his gracious purposes with or without us. Our obedience is important, but only as it fits into the bigger picture of God's loving work for the salvation of the world.

THE ADVANTAGES OF REMAINING SIN. John Newton coined the phrase "the advantages of remaining sin" to describe how God uses even our sin to accomplish his purposes for our good and his glory. In this week's passage, we see how God uses David's sinful census as the occasion for the sanctification of the future site of the temple. This is good news for those who know their own sinfulness: even our sin cannot defeat God's purposes but is instead part of his loving plan.

Whole-Bible Connections

THE DAVIDIC COVENANT. The covenant God makes with David is a new step forward in God's plan of redemptive history,[1] though it builds upon his previous covenants with Abraham and Moses. God had promised to give the land of Canaan to Abraham's descendants; this was accomplished in a preliminary way through Joshua, but the conquest of the land was left incomplete. Only through David is Israel finally given rest from their enemies in the land. God also promises that he will dwell with Israel in Jerusalem through the temple built by David's son Solomon. God's promise to dwell with his people will now be accomplished through an irrevocable commitment to David's dynasty.

JESUS, A MAN OF PEACE. We might think of David as the ideal king of ancient Israel, but according to the Chronicler there is a major issue: he is a man of violence. Even though the wars he fights are legitimate, there is still something inappropriate about God's chosen king being associated with bloodshed. As a man of peace, Solomon is the Chronicler's ideal king. This is a value embodied ultimately in Christ, who wins victory not through military might but through the weakness of submitting to death on a cross. Jesus finds a path to victory though weakness instead of human power and is exalted through humiliation. This marks him out as the even greater Son of David.

Theological Soundings

GOD'S FREEDOM. Given how important the building of the temple is in the overall story of the Bible, it may be surprising to see how negatively God reacts to David's initial desire to build it. The temple's status as an architectural feat built by men, along with its static confinement to one place, might tempt people to believe they could control God. In Jeremiah's day, the motto "the temple of the LORD" was the rallying cry of those who wrongly thought that God would protect Jerusalem and his temple regardless of whether or not his people actually obeyed him (Jer. 7:4). But God's freedom can never be limited or confined by human works; only by his own sovereign initiative and on his own terms can he be bound to us.

SPIRITUAL WARFARE. One of the main themes of this week's passage is how God gives his people victory in warfare through David. Although the kingdom of Jesus is not of this world, we are nevertheless just as much engaged in warfare as David was. According to Paul, our battle is "not . . . against flesh and blood, but against the . . . spiritual forces of evil" (Eph. 6:12). Although Christ has already won the definitive battle, triumphing over Satan at the cross, the war is still ongoing, and Christians should expect conflict if they follow Christ. As did those in David's day, we still look forward and fight toward the day when God will finally purge this world from sin and suffering and usher us into his promised rest.

Personal Implications

Take time to reflect on the implications of 1 Chronicles 17–22 for your own life today. Consider what you have learned that might lead you to praise God, repent of sin, and trust more deeply in his gracious promises. Write down your reflections under the three headings we have considered and on the passage as a whole.

1. Gospel Glimpses

2. Whole-Bible Connections

3. Theological Soundings

4. 1 Chronicles 17–22

> ## As You Finish This Unit . . .

Take a moment now to ask for the Lord's blessing and help as you continue in this study of 1–2 Chronicles. And take a moment also to look back through this unit of study, to reflect on some key things that the Lord may be teaching you.

Definition

[1] **Redemptive history** – The progressive unfolding in history of God's plan to redeem his people. God's purposes of redemption become clearer and more developed through his acts in history and through his successive revelation to Adam, Noah, Abraham, Moses, David, and the prophets, and in the New Testament.

WEEK 5: PREPARATIONS FOR THE TEMPLE

1 Chronicles 23–29

▲

The Chronicler continues to describe the preparation for the temple, emphasizing David's role in creating the blueprint for temple worship through God's inspiration. Chapters 23–27 give us the organization of personnel: the priests and Levites, along with the Levitical singers, gatekeepers, and officers, as well as the administrators of David's kingdom. Chapter 28 records a second charge of David to Solomon, where he entrusts Solomon with the temple plans in detail. In chapter 29, David enlists the people's help in donating to the cause of building the temple, and in accepting Solomon as their king. These chapters make it quite clear that, while Solomon is entrusted with building the temple, the plan for the temple is divinely revealed to David first of all.

The Big Picture

1 Chronicles 23–29 shows us God's revelation of his plan for worship in the temple, revealed through his servant David, and highlights the importance of the participation of all Israel in helping Solomon realize this plan.

> **Reflection and Discussion**

Read through the complete passage for this study, 1 Chronicles 23–29. Then review the questions below concerning this section of 1–2 Chronicles and write your notes on them. (For further background, see the *ESV Study Bible*, pages 735–742; available online at www.esv.org.)

1. The Organization of Personnel (23:1–27:34)

According to 23:2–6, David divides the Levites into a new organizational struc- ture that accounts for the three Levitical families and also makes use of the number 24 (12 x 2). The number 12 matches the number of months in a year and also reflects the number of tribes in Israel, for the Levites represent the whole people. Based on 23:25–26, what is the reason for this new organization?

Levitical singing is an entirely new institution not carried over from the Levites' tabernacle service. What do you think singing adds to the worship of God?

Consider 23:30–31 and notice the emphasis on time: the singing of the Levites continues every day and throughout all the seasons and festivals of the year. The praise of God in the temple is thus continual. How is the institution of singing a picture of the reality expressed in verse 25, that God will dwell in Jerusalem forever?

Consider 24:5, 31. The casting of lots is one way of seeking God's will in the Old Testament (and once in the New Testament; see Acts 1:26), and so the organizing of the priests and Levites is done according to God's plan. Notice the emphasis on "all alike" in these verses: the Levitical distribution includes everyone. How is this a picture of the unity that all Israel should share, according to the Chronicler? How should it influence how we think about worship?

Why are the remaining roles of the Levites in chapter 26 theologically important? What do the gatekeepers teach us about God's holiness? What does the oversight of the treasury teach us about how we should handle our resources? How does the involvement of the Levites in administrating the kingdom and instructing in "everything pertaining to God and for the affairs of the king" (v. 32) illustrate the importance of the unity of God's people?

Chapter 27 shows us the organization of the military and the whole people. In light of Exodus 19:6, what do you think is the significance of the repetition of the numbers 12 and 24, the same numbers used to organize the priests and

1 CHRONICLES 23-29

Levites? Consider verse 23: how is it an expression of faith not to count those under 20 years of age?

2. The Transfer of Power from David to Solomon (28:1–29:30)

Consider 28:4–10 and notice the repetition of the words "chose" and "chosen." Is God's promise to Solomon conditional or unconditional? How does the insistence on keeping God's commandments fit with the emphasis on God's election? Why are a "whole heart" and a "willing mind" (v. 9) so important?

According to 28:11, who should receive credit for the plan of the temple—Solomon or David? Based on 28:19, is David's plan for the temple something he designed on his own? Based on the earlier story about bringing up the ark, why is it important that God is ultimately the source for the plan of the temple? What are the implications of this for our worship?

In 29:1–5, David makes clear that neither he nor Solomon is able to do the work God has given them without the help of the whole people. In verses 5 and 9, how is the people's action described, and why is this important? How is the truth of the importance of human participation importantly qualified by David's prayer, especially in verse 14?

In verses 18–19, David asks God to keep in the people's hearts "such purposes and thoughts" as described in this chapter. What does this tell us about the connection between human will and God's sovereignty?

Read through the following three sections on *Gospel Glimpses, Whole-Bible Connections*, and *Theological Soundings*. Then take time to consider the *Personal Implications* these sections may have for you.

Gospel Glimpses

GOD DWELLS WITH HIS PEOPLE FOREVER. The transition from tabernacle to temple provides a picture of the enduring nature of God's commitment to us. The solidity of a stone structure pictures the fact that God has come to dwell with his people forever. This commitment of God depends on his eternal purpose and is not ultimately turned aside or thwarted by human failure or sin. Through many twists and turns, God remains faithful to his people and committed to redeem them from their sins.

GOD GIVES FIRST. Our relationship with God is not based on what we have given to him. Indeed, everything we might give to him he gave to us first, since all things belong ultimately to him. Thus our giving to God is a response to his kindness to us. To the extent that our hearts are captured by God's amazing beneficence to us, it is to that extent that we will desire to respond in worship to him. And yet even this willingness of our hearts is ultimately a gift from him. Salvation belongs to the Lord and is a gift from first to last.

Whole-Bible Connections

DAVID AND THE LEVITICAL SINGERS. The institution of song is a new development in redemptive history. No songs of the patriarchs are recorded, and under Moses and the judges, singing is only an occasional response to God's deliverance. But with David, song becomes a perpetual and central aspect of the worship of God, giving joyful expression to the willing, worshiping heart. The Chronicler describes this ministry of song as prophetic (1 Chron. 25:2–3), which gives us the historical background for the origin and divine inspiration of the book of Psalms.

CONDITIONAL OR UNCONDITIONAL? Is God's covenant with Israel based on his unconditional love, or does it depend on the people's obedience? This is a question that recurs throughout the Old Testament. As with all of the covenants, obedience is key, and Israel's disobedience leads to the disaster of exile. But, mysteriously, God remains committed to Israel despite her violation of the covenant. This tension is not resolved until the coming of Christ, who fulfills the conditions of the covenant on our behalf. Though obedience is still a necessary evidence of our salvation, we need not worry about meriting God's favor, since our legal standing in the covenant is grounded in Christ's fulfillment of its conditions.

Theological Soundings

FREE WILL AND DIVINE SOVEREIGNTY. It is important to affirm the reality of human free will, because it is crucial that our worship for God comes from a willing heart. God did not make us as robots; our ability to make choices is central to our humanity. However, our freedom does not mean that we are independent of God's sovereignty, nor does it mean that we are able to choose to abandon our sin without God's help, for our wills are held in bondage by sin. Our freedom to choose God depends on the prior work of the Holy Spirit in our hearts, opening our eyes and bringing us to Jesus. As Paul affirms in Ephesians 2:10, the good works we are called to walk in are those that God has prepared for us beforehand.

THE WORD DWELLS IN SONG. Singing has a central place in Christian worship. In Colossians 3:16, Paul describes it as the means by which the "word of Christ dwell[s] richly" in us, because in singing "spiritual songs," God's people demonstrate that his Spirit indwells each of them, so that all together they form one temple of God. In fact, Paul calls this singing "teaching and admonishing one another," because when we sing, each of us is in some sense a teacher of the others. As with the Levites, there is something prophetic about our singing, as we are called to bring God's Word to each other. And all of this is an expression of what ought to be in our hearts: "thankfulness . . . to God." Thus God's people, all ministering the Word of Christ to one another, by the power of the Spirit, with heartfelt thankfulness to God, are the true temple of the Lord.

Personal Implications

Take time to reflect on the implications of 1 Chronicles 23–29 for your own life today. Consider what you have learned that might lead you to praise God, repent of sin, and trust more deeply in his gracious promises. Write down your reflections under the three headings we have considered and on the passage as a whole.

1. Gospel Glimpses

2. Whole-Bible Connections

3. Theological Soundings

4. 1 Chronicles 23–29

As You Finish This Unit . . .

Take a moment now to ask for the Lord's blessing and help as you continue in this study of 1–2 Chronicles. And take a moment also to look back through this unit of study, to reflect on some key things that the Lord may be teaching you.

WEEK 6: BUILDING THE TEMPLE

2 Chronicles 1–5

▲

The Place of the Passage

Having described David's preparations for building the temple and the transition in kingship to Solomon, the Chronicler turns to a description of Solomon's faithful execution of the task with which he has been charged. Chapter 1 of 2 Chronicles describes Solomon's acquisition of the wisdom necessary for his task, while chapter 2 describes his alliance with Hiram of Tyre, who provides resources and skilled labor. Chapters 3–4 describe the actual construction of the temple and its furnishings, and chapter 5 outlines the preparations for dedicating the temple, preparing the reader for the dedication ceremony described in the following chapters.

The Big Picture

Second Chronicles 1–5 describes Solomon's faithfulness in executing David's plan, but more importantly, these chapters highlight God's faithfulness in fulfilling the promise made to David to establish David's son and to make his name dwell in Jerusalem through the construction of a temple.

Reflection and Discussion

Read through the complete passage for this study, 2 Chronicles 1–5. Then review the questions below concerning this section of 1–2 Chronicles and write your notes on them. (For further background, see the *ESV Study Bible*, pages 744–748; available online at www.esv.org.)

1. Wisdom and Wise Friends (1:1–2:18)

Compared to Saul, who "did not seek guidance from the Lord" (1 Chron. 10:14), how does Solomon begin his reign, in 2 Chronicles, chapter 1? What does Solomon's answer to God's offer (vv. 7–10) tell us about him? Compare this passage with Proverbs 3:13–18. Why is wisdom more valuable than anything else? Consider also Job 28. From where does wisdom come?

Remember the stories of the Ammonites and the Syrians, who opposed David in 1 Chronicles 19. Disaster awaits those who oppose God's anointed. In contrast, in 2 Chronicles 2 we see a model of Gentile support for God's king, which leads to blessing for Hiram of Tyre. Consider how Solomon and Hiram address each other (especially vv. 7, 8, and 15). Who is the more powerful member of this relationship? What does this say about how God has been working?

Compared to the portrayal of Huram-abi in Kings, the Chronicler has added material connecting him closely to Oholiab, the master-craftsman who worked on the tabernacle. The list of Huram-abi's skills in verse 14 has been expanded to include Oholiab's skills from Exodus 38:23, and whereas 1 Kings 7:14 notes that Huram-abi's mother was from Naphtali, Chronicles traces his genealogy among the Danites, the tribe of Oholiab. (In 1 Kings, Huram-abi is called "Hiram"—not to be confused with the king by that name.) Given the mention of Bezalel in

43

1:5, the Chronicler seems to be connecting Solomon and Huram-abi to the two artificers of the tabernacle, Bezalel and Oholiab. Why do you think establishing continuity between the tabernacle and the temple is so important to the Chronicler? What impact should this continuity have on Israel's worship and faith?

-----

2. The Construction of the Temple (3:1–5:14)

The plans for the temple in chapter 3 invite us to reflect on the theological meaning signified by the temple's architecture. The journey from the outer court to the nave, and from the nave to the Most Holy Place, traces ascending levels of holiness. Walls, doors, and the veil separate the people from God's glory and guard the temple from contamination by the unclean. Glimmering gold, and blue, purple, and crimson cloth represent the shining glory of God's presence in the heavens, and the cherubim[1] depicted everywhere represent his military might while barring the way to his presence. The pillars stationed outside have names evoking permanence and strength and communicating the design of the temple to be a lasting place for God to dwell. How does this theme of God's holiness and his *inaccessibility* fit with his commitment to be *present* with his people?

In chapter 4, the equipment of the temple is described. The altar reminds us of the need for blood atonement for the forgiveness of sins if God is to dwell with his people. What is the purpose of the sea and the basins (v. 6)? How do these elements communicate the need for purification in approaching God? What do the lampstands represent? What about the bread of the Presence?

In chapter 5, the construction and furnishing of the temple is finally completed. The ark—the sign of God's presence—is brought into the sanctuary, sacrifices are offered, and music and worship ring out, but something is still missing until the last verse, when the temple is filled with the cloud of God's glory. The cloud of glory demonstrates God's sovereign choice to make the temple his dwelling place. Of what other event(s) in the Bible does this remind you? In what ways? Why is this manifestation of the cloud so important?

Read through the following three sections on *Gospel Glimpses, Whole-Bible Connections,* and *Theological Soundings.* Then take time to consider the *Personal Implications* these sections may have for you.

Gospel Glimpses

GOD GIVES WISDOM. While the Bible calls us to seek after wisdom, it also affirms that wisdom is not something we can acquire merely by our own efforts. In fact, human wisdom is foolish compared to true, godly wisdom. Wisdom is given freely by God. In this, as with so many things, God delights to give freely what we could never gain for ourselves. This is good news for us, because life is complex and treacherous, and discerning how to make good choices is often beyond our ability. But we can turn in faith to God and ask him for the wisdom to make it through each day.

THE GLORY AND THE BLOOD. The gold and the lights of the temple are a picture of God's glory, the ultimate beauty for which our hearts were created. The phenomenal majesty and beauty of the temple's architecture points us to the reality that the God who dwells in the temple is more beautiful than the earthly things that captivate our hearts. But how can we come to God when we are sinners, with defiled hearts? The water of purification and the blood of the altar point the way to God's forgiveness and provision of atonement. God has made a way for us to be purified of our sins, so that we can come into his courts with praise, and our hearts can find rest in him. That way is through his Son, Jesus Christ, who was sacrificed on the cross for our sins and who rose again on the third day and now makes intercession for us.

Whole-Bible Connections

CHRIST THE WISDOM OF GOD. The Old Testament makes clear the importance of wisdom: in order to obey God and live life well, we need his gift of wisdom to interpret reality and know how to act. Drawing on the personification of Wisdom in Proverbs, the New Testament specifically identifies Christ as the Wisdom of God (1 Cor. 1:24, 30). This is not merely because Christ is our wise teacher (although he *is* that) but because he is the incarnation of God's wisdom; his life and especially his death, which seem foolish to the world, are in fact God's skillful achievement of goodness, happiness, and everlasting life. In Christ, God grants his wisdom to us, teaching us to turn away from the death of sin and toward life in him.

THE NEW JERUSALEM. The theological architecture of Solomon's temple is a picture of what it means to live in God's presence. In the New Testament, this imagery is taken up in the description of the future new Jerusalem of Revelation 21, in which God's people will dwell with him. In John's vision of this city, there is no temple (Rev. 21:22), because the "temple" has expanded to comprise the whole city, which is covered with gold and jewels and is a perfect cube, the shape of the Most Holy Place. The city shines with God's glory, but there are no longer any walls separating the people from God, nor is there an altar; instead, the Lamb who has been given as the final sacrifice dwells there. And instead of the sea, a river flows out from the city, symbolizing life in the Spirit, which comes to the world from Christ's work.

Theological Soundings

REVELATION AND KNOWLEDGE. Wisdom is God's gift—we are dependent on God for knowledge just as much as we are for our very being. We may be used to thinking of the revelation of God in Scripture as the sole way in which he imparts knowledge, but in fact all of our knowledge comes from him. Our own reasoning processes do not operate autonomously, apart from God; rather, we can know successfully only if his Spirit gives us the ability to know. So, in a sense, all of our knowledge is revelation. Still, we should distinguish between general revelation, the general knowledge of creation that all humans have in some measure; and special revelation, the knowledge necessary for salvation that God grants through his Spirit.

THE CHURCH AS GOD'S TEMPLE. The New Testament applies the imagery of the temple to the church; thus it is important to understand the temple in order to grasp how the church ought to operate. As he did in the temple, God's Spirit dwells in us: thus we are precious in God's sight, and an attack on us is an attack on God's holiness (1 Cor. 3:16–17). This also means that we are obliged to be holy and to avoid idolatry (1 Cor. 6:19; 2 Cor. 6:14–18). This truth is applicable not only to individuals; rather, God's people together form the temple, all supporting one another as individual stones and beams, with the apostles and prophets as the foundation and Jesus as the cornerstone (Eph. 2:20–22).

> ## Personal Implications

Take time to reflect on the implications of 2 Chronicles 1–5 for your own life today. Consider what you have learned that might lead you to praise God, repent of sin, and trust more deeply in his gracious promises. Write down your reflections under the three headings we have considered and on the passage as a whole.

1. Gospel Glimpses

2. Whole-Bible Connections

3. Theological Soundings

4. 2 Chronicles 1–5

As You Finish This Unit . . .

Take a moment now to ask for the Lord's blessing and help as you continue in this study of 1–2 Chronicles. And take a moment also to look back through this unit of study, to reflect on some key things that the Lord may be teaching you.

Definition

[1] **Cherub (pl. cherubim)** – A type of angel that typically accompanies God's presence. In Scripture these figures are terrifying guardians who reflect God's power and threaten to strike down anyone who would transgress his holy place; thus it is one of the cherubim who bars the way to the garden of Eden with a flaming sword (Gen. 3:24). In a way, the cherubim are the heavenly equivalent of the Levitical gatekeepers.

Week 7: Temple Dedication and the Greatness of Solomon

2 Chronicles 6–9

▲

Chapters 6–9 are the climax of 1–2 Chronicles: everything that has gone before serves as preparation for Solomon's blessing and prayer to God in chapter 6 and God's answer in chapter 7. Chapter 8 then lists several other examples of Solomon's greatness, which are further fulfillments of God's promise to David. Chapter 9 demonstrates Solomon's great wisdom through his encounter with the Queen of Sheba, who tests him, and the chapter concludes with a description of Solomon's fantastic wealth and his death. With the conclusion of these chapters, David and Solomon stand together as the Chronicler's ideal portrait of kingly leadership. They provide the standard for the rest of the book.

The Big Picture

In answer to Solomon's prayer, God commits to making the temple in Jerusalem a place of blessing for the people of Israel, especially concerning the forgiveness of sin, and he continues to bless Solomon throughout the rest of his life.

Read through the complete passage for this study, 2 Chronicles 6–9. Then review the questions below concerning this section of 1–2 Chronicles and write your notes on them. (For further background, see the *ESV Study Bible*, pages 749–756; available online at www.esv.org.)

1. The Temple Dedication (6:1–7:22)

In 6:1–2, Solomon tells his hearers that the Lord has said he will dwell in thick darkness,[1] yet Solomon has built him a place in which to dwell. What would it mean for God to dwell in darkness, and how is this different from dwelling in the temple? Does the temple cancel out God's hiddenness, or is there an abiding tension here?

Chapter 6 emphasizes God's fulfilling his promises (see especially vv. 10, 14–15). What is the connection between God's promise to make his name dwell in Jerusalem and his promise to make David's heirs into kings? How are other promises God made to Abraham and to David also fulfilled in his faithfulness to Solomon?

If Solomon knows that God is faithful to fulfill his promises, and has seen evidence of this, why does he still ask God to fulfill his promises (6:16–17)? Is this a picture of how we should pray?

If the temple is a place in which God may dwell (6:2), why does Solomon question whether God can dwell there (v. 18)? For that matter, if even heaven and the highest heaven cannot contain God, why is heaven called his dwelling place (v. 21)? What does it mean to say that God is "present" in his temple?

Consider the possible sorts of prayers that Solomon mentions in chapter 6. Why is there such an emphasis on sin, repentance, and forgiveness in the people's relationship to God (consider especially v. 36)? Consider verses 36–40: what would these verses mean to the Chronicler's audience, on the other side of the exile? What might verse 42 mean for them?

Consider 6:32–33. What is Solomon implying about how Gentiles should relate to Israel? What does this say about how God's plan for Israel fits into his plan for the whole world?

What is the significance of the fire coming down from heaven in 7:1–3? Can you think of other examples in the Bible of fire coming down from heaven? Is the temple an expression merely of David's and Solomon's good ideas, or does God endorse it too?

What does God's response to Solomon in 7:12–22 add to our understanding of the theological significance of the temple? What do verses 13–14 tell us about how God relates to his people? How do verses 19–22 importantly qualify the idea of the permanence of the temple as an expression of God's eternal love?

2. Solomon's Wealth and Wisdom (8:1–9:31)

Second Chronicles 8:1–10 tells us more about how Solomon fulfills God's promise to give his people rest in the land. Consider the mention of Hamath in the description of the ideal northern border of Israel in Numbers 34:8. How does this background help us understand the significance of 2 Chronicles 8:3–4? What do verses 7–8 imply about how Solomon's kingship connects to the conquest led by Joshua? Are Solomon's actions different from that conquest in any way?

How is the interaction between Solomon and the Queen of Sheba an illustration of how Israel should relate to the Gentiles? What does the Queen of Sheba learn about Israel's God (9:8–9)?

Read through the following three sections on *Gospel Glimpses*, *Whole-Bible Connections*, and *Theological Soundings*. Then take time to consider the *Personal Implications* these sections may have for you.

> ## Gospel Glimpses

REPENTANCE AND FORGIVENESS. Solomon's prayer shows us just how central repentance and forgiveness are to our life with God. There is no one without sin, but the good news is that God has made a way for us to be in his presence. He atones for our sins through the work of Christ, so that we can repent of our sins and come to him. Because of Christ's work, God's ears are always open to our cries for help. This pattern of repentance and forgiveness is not just something we follow when we first become Christians; rather, it is to be the regular pattern of the Christian life. As we grow in knowledge of our sin, we are to return continually to God for forgiveness. And we will always find him eager to meet us with his love.

GOD'S PRESENCE. The temple witnesses to God's commitment to be with his people. Despite their sin and waywardness, God covenants to be their God and to dwell with them. The permanence of the temple testifies to the enduring nature of God's commitment to remain with his people. The greatest gift God can give us is himself, and there is nothing we should desire more than to be with him. This is not something we can make happen purely through our own efforts; rather, God must choose to come to us. The entrance of the cloud of glory into the temple shows that God has done just that: he has freely chosen to dwell with his people.

Whole-Bible Connections

SAMUEL–KINGS AND CHRONICLES. The portrayal of David and Solomon in Chronicles avoids mention of the great sins of their lives. We do not find the narrative of David and Bathsheba (2 Samuel 11), nor do we hear of Solomon's fall into idolatry (1 Kings 11). This is not because the Chronicler is trying to deceive his audience or conceal these facts from them—they knew of these events from Samuel and Kings already. Rather, the Chronicler focuses on David and Solomon as ideals and so emphasizes their successes as a model of how a good king should behave.

THE TEMPLE TORN DOWN. In this narrative of the dedication of the temple, we also see a foreshadowing that God's temple will one day be torn down because of the people's sins. Jesus refers to this theme of the destruction and rebuilding of the temple in John 2:18–22, where he says, "Destroy this temple, and in three days I will raise it up," referring to his own body. Jesus' body is the fulfillment of the Old Testament temple: "in him the whole fullness of deity dwells bodily" (Col. 2:9). In other words, Jesus is Immanuel, "God with us"—the ultimate expression of God's commitment to be with his people by taking on their humanity in the person of Christ.

ONE GREATER THAN SOLOMON. In Matthew 12:42, Jesus tells his hearers, "The queen of the South will rise up at the judgment with this generation and condemn it, for she came from the ends of the earth to hear the wisdom of Solomon, and behold, something greater than Solomon is here." The Queen of Sheba is a type of the Gentiles who embrace Jesus even though his own people have rejected him. The wise men who come to him bearing precious gifts in Matthew's Gospel are an example of this. As the Wisdom of God incarnate, the King who will bring his people ultimate rest, Jesus is even greater than Solomon, and he fulfills in an ultimate way God's promise to David of a future king.

Theological Soundings

GOD'S OMNIPRESENCE. Solomon's address at the temple dedication is crucial for understanding who God is. When we say that God is omnipresent, we mean that he has no spatial limitations—nothing can contain him (2 Chron. 6:18).

Language in Scripture speaking of God's presence should not be understood in a way that contradicts this basic commitment. When we speak of God as present in a particular locality, we mean that his normally invisible presence is specially manifested to us by visible signs, such as fire and smoke. In the case of the temple, God's presence there means that he is committed to hearing the prayers of his people toward the temple and to honoring the sacrifices made there.

THE INCARNATION. Just as God's presence in the temple is not to be understood as a spatial limitation on him, neither can we understand the incarnation in this way. When the Son becomes man, he does not cease to be God, nor is his divinity in any way lessened. As the eternal second person of the Trinity, he continues to fill all time and space as the Divine Word. Otherwise, he would not be able to unite us to the true God. Instead, the fullness of who God is dwells in Jesus. Because of this, Jesus can promise to be with us always, even though his body remains in heaven, seated at the right hand of the Father. In fact, it is precisely because God is omnipresent that he is able to be always with us, loving and keeping us by virtue of his Son's incarnation, death, and resurrection.

Personal Implications

Take time to reflect on the implications of 2 Chronicles 6–9 for your own life today. Consider what you have learned that might lead you to praise God, repent of sin, and trust more deeply in his gracious promises. Write down your reflections under the three headings we have considered and on the passage as a whole.

1. Gospel Glimpses

2. Whole-Bible Connections

3. Theological Soundings

4. 2 Chronicles 6–9

As You Finish This Unit . . .

Take a moment now to ask for the Lord's blessing and help as you continue in this study of 1–2 Chronicles. And take a moment also to look back through this unit of study, to reflect on some key things that the Lord may be teaching you.

Definition

[1] **Darkness** – Visible manifestations of God's presence in the Bible are often accompanied by clouds and darkness (see Ps. 18:11) as a reminder that God's true being is always beyond the grasp of what we can see or comprehend.

Week 8: Rehoboam, Abijah, and Asa

2 Chronicles 10–16

▲

The Chronicler has established David and Solomon as norms of kingship, as those who inquire of the Lord, follow his law, support true worship, and prosper as a result. From here, the Chronicler begins to lead the reader through Israel's subsequent history of kings whose record is more mixed. Rehoboam (chapters 10–12) loses the northern kingdom through his folly, and, despite early obedience, he sins and is punished by an invasion. Abijah (chapter 13) obeys the Lord and enjoys military success. Asa (chapters 14–16) reforms worship, but near the end of his reign he turns away from the Lord and is afflicted with a foot disease. There is no strong element of progression or development through these stories; rather, the Chronicler wants us to learn from each individual generation.

The Big Picture

The reigns of Rehoboam, Abijah, and Asa underscore the fact that the lives of most kings include periods of faithfulness as well as periods of rebellion, and God brings either rewards or afflictions as a result.

> ## Reflection and Discussion

Read through the complete passage for this study, 2 Chronicles 10–16. Then review the questions below concerning this section of 1–2 Chronicles and write your notes on them. (For further background, see the *ESV Study Bible*, pages 756–764; available online at www.esv.org.)

1. Rehoboam (10:1–12:16)

In chapter 10, why does Rehoboam listen to the advice of the younger men rather than that of the older men? How does his wisdom compare to his father's? According to verse 15, what is the ultimate reason for what transpires in this chapter?

Who is "Israel" in 10:16? Who is "Israel" in 10:17? Why do you think the Chronicler juxtaposes these two definitions of Israel? Is one group more truly "Israel" than the other, and if so, what is it that makes this the case?

In 11:4, what two reasons are given as to why Rehoboam should not wage war on the northern kingdom, even though he is the rightful king? What does this say about the caution necessary before going to war? What does Rehoboam's response say about him, and what strategy does he pursue instead?

Consider 11:13–17. Why do the priests and the Levites leave the northern kingdom and come to Judah? How might this speak to the Chronicler's first audience, in a context in which the inhabitants of surrounding nations were often hostile to Judah and the worship at the temple in Jerusalem?

According to 12:1, why does Rehoboam abandon God's law? What are the consequences? Why does God mitigate his punishment in verses 6–8? In light of 1 Chronicles 21:13, what does it mean when God says in verse 8, "They shall be servants to him, that they may know my service and the service of the kingdoms of the countries"?

2. Abijah (13:1–22)

According to Abijah's speech in 13:6–7, why did the northern kingdom separate from Judah? Consider verses 8–12: what is the difference between Israel and Judah in this passage? What does this say about the importance of worshiping God correctly, and its connection to success in Judah's warfare? According to verse 18, why do the men of Judah win the battle?

3. Asa (14:1–16:14)

According to 14:2–5, how does Asa show his obedience to God? How is this connected to his prosperity and the size of his army in verses 5–8? Notice the theme of "help" appearing again in verse 11. Why does Asa prevail against the Ethiopians?

The opening of Azariah's prophecy in 15:2 is a good summary of one of the Chronicler's most important principles. How do verses 3–7 flesh out this principle? What is Asa's response to the prophecy in verses 8–16? What does verse 17 say about the limitations of his success?

Consider 16:2–3. What do Asa's actions say about the source of his trust? How do his actions make sense from a worldly, strategic perspective? How does Asa respond to Hanani's prophecy in verse 10, and what does this tell us about how far he has fallen? How does Asa's reaction to his disease in verse 12 compare to Rehoboam's reaction to Shishak's invasion in 12:6?

Read through the following three sections on *Gospel Glimpses*, *Whole-Bible Connections*, and *Theological Soundings*. Then take time to consider the *Personal Implications* these sections may have for you.

Gospel Glimpses

SERVING GOD VERSUS SERVING MEN. Rehoboam and the people of Israel in his time learn the hard way about the difference between serving men and serving God. We may think of obeying God as the hard way, but in fact it is the way that brings blessing. When we declare independence from God, we end up enslaved to things that are not God, and such things always prove to be harsh taskmasters. Perhaps we sometimes imagine God as if he were like some of the more judgmental and harsh human "masters" we may have experienced. But the good news is that we have a God who knows our weakness and forgives our sin. Those who come to him like the Prodigal Son, glad to be a slave in his household, will discover that he greets them with open arms and accepts them as his own children.

JESUS' PERFECT OBEDIENCE. The lives of Rehoboam and Asa provide examples of men who begin to follow God's law but are tempted and turn aside from this pursuit. This highlights the difficulty of persevering in obedience. As Solomon prayed at the temple dedication, "There is no one who does not sin" (2 Chron. 6:36). But the good news of the gospel is that there is someone who remained perfectly faithful to God. Jesus Christ obeyed God perfectly, every moment of every day, in every thought, word, and deed. He is the king who finally fulfills and even exceeds the pattern set by David and Solomon. And this perfect obedience is given to us, as his righteousness is imputed to us in our justification. Because we are in him, we need not fear that our sin will be the end of the story.

Whole-Bible Connections

KINGS AND CHRONICLES. The Chronicler brings a different perspective on Israel's rulers than do 1–2 Kings. Except for Abijah, who receives a purely positive evaluation in Chronicles, the Chronicler tends to complicate the picture of who these kings were. According to Kings, Rehoboam did evil in the eyes of the Lord, while Asa did good. But the Chronicler zooms in much closer to show us periods of both obedience and disobedience for both of these kings. While Kings is interested in the big-picture trajectory of Israel toward exile, the Chronicler wants us to see the moral complexity of these kings' lives and to realize that a one-time commitment to God is not enough; true obedience requires that we persevere throughout our lifetime. The books of Kings and Chronicles have different perspectives because they have different aims in telling the story; like the four Gospels, these different perspectives are complementary and give us a richness of insight we would not have from just one narrative alone.

THE YOKE OF JESUS. Rehoboam learned the hard way what it means to serve men rather than God. The irony is that the whole trouble started because he made it hard for his subjects to serve him. In hindsight, his "heavy yoke" (2 Chron. 10:14) policy was a poor idea; more importantly, it was unkind and unloving, unlike the elders' advice to "be good" to the people (v. 7). How different is Jesus! In Matthew 11:28–30, Christ tells us that his yoke is easy and his burden is light. This is because he is a man gentle and lowly in heart, and he calls those who labor and are heavy burdened to come to him for rest. What a contrast is the wise kindness of Jesus to the folly of Rehoboam.

▶ Theological Soundings

IDOLATRY. The establishment of calf worship by Jeroboam and the reform of Asa bring the problem of idolatry into focus for the first time in 1–2 Chronicles. Idolatry involves more than worshiping other gods besides the true God; it also involves worshiping the true God according to our own imaginations rather than in the way he has commanded. After all, Jeroboam was still worshiping the Lord; he merely added calves and non-Levite priests—which is precisely the problem. All sin has an idolatrous aspect, for sin involves a distorted view of God that leads us to put something that is not God in his place.

PERSEVERANCE OF THE SAINTS. How do we fit the Chronicler's statement that "the LORD is with you while you are with him" (2 Chron. 15:2) with the doctrine that true saints do not fall away from the faith? It is true that God's grace is irresistible and that no one can snatch his elect away from him, but this does not mean that perseverance is unnecessary. Rather, God redeems his saints by changing their hearts and turning them toward himself throughout the course of their lives. This infallible divine plan even includes our sin; God may leave believers to themselves for a time in order to experience their own sinfulness and therefore their need of him. In these periods, there is a sense in which believers suffer God's absence, and thus experience what the Chronicler teaches. But from an ultimate perspective, God is still working in their lives, and he will use even these times of hardening to bring them closer to himself in the end.

▶ Personal Implications

Take time to reflect on the implications of 2 Chronicles 10–16 for your own life today. Consider what you have learned that might lead you to praise God, repent of sin, and trust more deeply in his gracious promises. Write down your reflections under the three headings we have considered and on the passage as a whole.

1. Gospel Glimpses

----

2. Whole-Bible Connections

3. Theological Soundings

4. 2 Chronicles 10–16

> ## As You Finish This Unit . . .

Take a moment now to ask for the Lord's blessing and help as you continue in this study of 1–2 Chronicles. And take a moment also to look back through this unit of study, to reflect on some key things that the Lord may be teaching you.

WEEK 9: JEHOSHAPHAT

2 Chronicles 17–20

▲

After relating the failure of Asa in his old age, the Chronicler introduces us to Asa's son Jehoshaphat. The story of Jehoshaphat is significantly expanded here from the version we find in Kings; clearly the Chronicler wants us to pay attention to this king. Despite some failings, Jehoshaphat is a model for the Chronicler of a king who walks in the ways of David and Solomon. Jehoshaphat reforms Judah's worship and responds to difficulty in his life by calling out to the Lord for help.

The Big Picture

The Chronicler shows us Jehoshaphat as an example of a king who brings people back to the Lord, reforms worship, establishes justice, and depends on the Lord's help; although he sins by allying himself with God's enemy, the overall pattern of Jehoshaphat's life is dependence on God, and he is blessed as a result.

Reflection and Discussion

Read through the complete passage for this study, 2 Chronicles 17–20. Then review the questions below concerning this section of 1–2 Chronicles and write your notes on them. (For further background, see the *ESV Study Bible*, pages 764–770; available online at www.esv.org.)

1. Reforms and Bad Friends (17:1–18:34)

According to 17:3–5, why does the Lord establish the kingdom in Jehoshaphat's hand? How do verses 7–9 reflect the Chronicler's ideal of the whole people's obeying God? What role does God's law play in this ideal? What do we learn about how this ideal might be accomplished, and the importance of good leadership for this task?

Consider the evidences of Jehoshaphat's greatness listed in 17:10–19. What do we learn about his relationship to surrounding Gentiles? What was the total sum of soldiers in Jehoshaphat's army? Keep in mind that numbers represent God's blessing in Chronicles. How does Jehoshaphat compare to the kings who have come before him?

Note Jehoshaphat's insistence on inquiring of the Lord (18:4–6). What does this say about him? What does it say about Ahab? What does this suggest about whether Ahab is the sort of person with whom Jehoshaphat should be making an alliance?

What does the messenger's advice in verse 12 suggest about why all the other prophets agree? How does Micaiah's advice show that he is different?

In verse 16, Micaiah invokes the dire image of scattered sheep without a shepherd[1] but gives it a positive twist by saying, "Let each return to his home in peace." What does this imply about the quality of the master they have lost? What do verses 20–22 imply about the Lord's attitude toward Ahab and the chances of a successful endeavor? How do these verses invert the significance of the other prophecies?

Why is Jehoshaphat rescued from the disaster Ahab's scheme brings upon him (vv. 31–32)? Why do you think Ahab's scheme fails to save him (v. 33)? In what ways are you tempted to rely on your own schemes, rather than on God? What does this whole episode teach us about God's sovereignty?

----

2. Justice and Deliverance (19:1–20:37)

What is the nature of Jehoshaphat's sin, according to Jehu (19:2)? How is this sinfulness mitigated (v. 3)?

Consider Jehoshaphat's vision for judicial reform as he expresses it in verses 6–7 and 9–11. What does this tell us about what justice should look like? What does it say about how justice and the role of a judge relates to God? According to verse 10, what are the chief things that must be carefully understood and discerned in order to be a faithful judge?

In 20:3–4, what is Jehoshaphat's response when he is threatened with disaster? Consider verses 6–10: what attributes of God does Jehoshaphat appeal to? what historical acts of God? How does the temple fit into his request for help?

According to God's answer in verses 15–17, what is he going to do? What is the people's part in their salvation? What role does faith play in the people's deliverance (v. 20)? What role does worship play (vv. 21–22)?

How is Jehoshaphat like Solomon, according to verses 29–30? How is he different from Solomon, according to verses 35–37? Why does his trade expedition fail, unlike Solomon's collaborative effort with Hiram to send ships to Ophir and Tarshish?

_____

_____

_____

_____

_____

Read through the following three sections on *Gospel Glimpses*, *Whole-Bible Connections*, and *Theological Soundings*. Then take time to consider the *Personal Implications* these sections may have for you.

Gospel Glimpses

GOD SAVES US FROM OURSELVES. Despite his overall concern to obey God, Jehoshaphat is enticed into sin by Ahab, and this almost gets him killed. But because he cries out to the Lord, he is delivered from his calamity. Much of our own suffering is self-caused, but the good news is that God delights to deliver us from the consequences of our sin. Even if our situation is entirely our own fault, if we turn to God in repentance he is quick to forgive and to save us from ourselves.

GOD FIGHTS THE BATTLE. The Chronicler emphasizes that Israel's military victory depends on God's help, but with Jehoshaphat we see the most complete expression of this truth; God's people are called merely to believe and to watch God deliver them. They do not strike a single blow; they merely collect the plunder afterward. This is a model that recurs in other visions of God's deliverance of his people: with Gog and Magog in Ezekiel 38–39, and with the defeat of the beast in Revelation 19. Our salvation does not depend on us or our strength but on the all-surpassing might of God—and if God is for us, who can stand against us (compare Rom. 8:31–39)?

Whole-Bible Connections

FAITH AND MARRIAGE. Jehoshaphat's unfaithfulness begins with a marriage allying him with an enemy of God. The danger of being drawn away from faith through marriage was a big concern in the postexilic community (see Ezra 10; Neh. 13:23–27). This is not a racist concern; rather, it has deeply religious motivations: wives who do not love the Lord and instead worship other gods will lead their husbands astray. Paul echoes the same concern when he says in 2 Corinthians 6:14–18 that believers should not be "unequally yoked" with unbelievers. This is not a concern only for marriage; it applies to all of our relationships. It is not that we should have no contact with unbelievers; rather, we should be careful concerning the people with whom we form the most central relationships in our lives, seeking to ensure that such people are pointing us toward God and not away from him.

TRUE AND FALSE PROPHECY. The campaign of Jehoshaphat and Ahab demonstrates the general biblical truth that false prophecy is dangerous and God's people must be discerning in listening to prophets. Deuteronomy 18:20–22 warns Israel to discern false prophecy and explains how to do so. But the true prophets of the Lord were nevertheless usually in the minority in Israel's history. The people preferred to listen to prophets who told them what they wanted to hear, while true prophets often had to endure rejection and mistreatment, as does Micaiah. This pattern culminates in Jesus, who, despite being the ultimate prophet, is rejected by his people and even killed because of his message.

Theological Soundings

PROVIDENCE. The bow seemingly drawn at random that strikes down Ahab is a classic example of God's providence. Even random events accomplish God's purposes and are under his control. Micaiah's vision of the heavenly court expounds a strong view of divine providence: God is sovereign even over deceiving spirits. The fact that God predestines everything that comes to pass is the basis for Paul's affirmation that all things work together for the good of God's elect (Rom. 8:28). We must make a few important qualifications, however: In God's providence, he is never guilty of sin—he does not tempt anyone (James 1:13). And although God's predestination extends even to the actions of humans, this does not mean that they become robots; God's predestination respects the secondary causes he has established and the real choices his creatures make. These qualifications should never be understood as a limitation on God's sovereignty; rather, they describe the way in which he sovereignly rules the world.

GOD'S JUSTICE. Jehoshaphat's reform highlights the importance of justice to God. The prophets' condemnations are focused not only on the problem of idolatry but also on the problem of the oppression of the weak and the failure of justice. Justice does not accept bribes and it shows no partiality, avoiding the special danger of favoritism toward the rich that leads to mistreatment of the poor (James 2:1–9). Justice also requires attention to God's law and fairness in applying it—to punish too severely is equally as unjust as being too lenient. Those in government have a special responsibility to represent God's justice, and Christian citizens have a duty to pray for them, and to seek justice in their own relationships and communities.

▶ **Personal Implications**

Take time to reflect on the implications of 2 Chronicles 17–20 for your own life today. Consider what you have learned that might lead you to praise God, repent of sin, and trust more deeply in his gracious promises. Write down your reflections under the three headings we have considered and on the passage as a whole.

1. Gospel Glimpses

2. Whole-Bible Connections

3. Theological Soundings

4. 2 Chronicles 17–20

As You Finish This Unit . . .

Take a moment now to ask for the Lord's blessing and help as you continue in this study of 1–2 Chronicles. And take a moment also to look back through this unit of study, to reflect on some key things that the Lord may be teaching you.

Definition

[1] **Shepherd** – The task of herding sheep was very familiar in ancient Israel, but the role of shepherd was also a popular metaphor for kingship throughout the ancient Near East.

WEEK 10: JEHORAM TO JOTHAM

2 Chronicles 21–27

▲

The Place of the Passage

Despite Jehoshaphat's righteousness, his successors follow in the steps of the house of Ahab. Jehoram murders his brothers and champions idolatry. His son Ahaziah dies giving military assistance to Joram, son of Ahab; Ahaziah's mother, Athaliah, who is Ahab's daughter, slaughters the royal family. However, the priest Jehoiada preserves one son, Joash, alive, and manages to overthrow Athaliah and put the rightful king on the throne. While Jehoiada is alive, Joash walks in the way of the Lord and repairs the temple, but after Jehoiada's death he turns away, going to the extreme of murdering Jehoiada's son Zechariah. Josiah's son Amaziah follows God only in a halfhearted manner, becoming enticed into worshiping Edomite gods. Uzziah lives a righteous and successful life, but near the end he violates the sanctity of the temple and is struck with a skin disease. His son Jotham walks in the ways of the Lord and is blessed.

The Big Picture

In this section, the Chronicler highlights God's commitment to his promise in preserving the house of David from near extinction and stresses the importance of listening to godly counsel.

Reflection and Discussion

Read through the complete passage for this study, 2 Chronicles 21–27. Then review the questions below concerning this section of 1–2 Chronicles and write your notes on them. (For further background, see the *ESV Study Bible*, pages 770–779; available online at www.esv.org.)

1. Jehoram, Ahaziah, and Athaliah (21:1–22:12)

In 21:2–3, what does Jehoshaphat do for his sons? How does Jehoram treat his brothers in verse 4? Why does he do this (v. 6), and what does this say about the importance of godly counsel? What are the consequences of this sin?

What does verse 7 tell us about God's commitment to the house of David? What are the consequences of Jehoram's actions in the rest of the narrative? What do the details of his funeral and burial say about him (v. 20)?

Consider 22:2–6. Whose influence leads Ahaziah into sin? What are the consequences of his sin (vv. 7–9)? Ahab and Jehoshaphat were Ahaziah's grandfathers: which does he resemble more?

With the death of Ahaziah, and Athaliah's bloody ascent to power, Judah is now ruled by a daughter of the house of Omri. Notice from 24:7 that Athaliah worships Baal, the favorite deity of her family. But Athaliah's intentions are thwarted by a courageous woman: based on verse 11, why do you think Jehosha-beath takes this risky action?

----

2. Joash (23:1–24:27)

Consider all the people involved in Jehoiada's scheme in 23:1–7. How does this illustrate the Chronicler's theme of the importance of individual commitment to supporting God's chosen king? In 23:13, the Chronicler specially emphasizes the presence of "all the people," and we find them worshiping and singing to God. Is this an odd time to be worshiping (in the middle of a coup)? What does this say about the importance of worship?

In verse 14, why does Jehoiada insist that Athaliah not be killed in the temple courts? Verse 21 tells us that the land experiences peace (ESV "quiet"); what do verses 16–20 tell us about what is necessary for such peace?

What does 24:2 say about the importance of good counsel? Based on verses 4–7, who dropped the ball in the project to restore the temple? What does Joash do in verses 8–14 to resolve the problem? What do the details of Jehoiada's burial in verse 16 say about him?

In 24:17–19, who influences Joash to take the actions he pursues? In the end, Joash falls into the bloodthirsty ways of Athaliah's line. How does Joash meet his end (vv. 23–24)? How is this poetic justice?

3. Amaziah, Uzziah, and Jotham (25:1–27:9)

Amaziah's refusal to execute the children of the conspirators in 25:4 shows how different he is from Athaliah. How does this illustrate the Chronicler's emphasis that God doesn't punish future generations for the sins of past generations?

Consider 25:5–13. Why is it a bad idea for Amaziah to hire mercenaries from Israel? What does it tell us about him that he listens to the voice of the prophet? Consider also verses 14–16. Why is Amaziah's decision to worship the gods of Edom foolish? How does he respond to God's prophet this time, and what do these verses say about Amaziah's willingness to listen to counsel?

Notice that the issue of listening comes up again in 25:20. What is Amaziah's central character flaw? What are its consequences?

What are the results of Uzziah's obedience in 26:6–15? In verse 16, what character trait leads to his downfall? What does this downfall say about the importance of worshiping God properly? How can our pride get in the way of proper worship?

According to 27:6, why is Jotham a successful king?

Read through the following three sections on *Gospel Glimpses*, *Whole-Bible Connections*, and *Theological Soundings*. Then take time to consider the *Personal Implications* these sections may have for you.

Gospel Glimpses

DELIVER US FROM EVIL. Jehoram, Ahaziah, and Athaliah are some of the most evil characters in the entire Bible. In this passage, we see God's commitment to the line of David confronted by the human propensity for carnage and bloodshed. Yet, despite the darkness, the spark of David's line is not wiped out; God's purposes cannot be thwarted by human evil. Every mortal plot and scheme ends ultimately where Athaliah's does: disaster. But those who trust in the Lord can have a sure hope that God ultimately will deliver them from the schemes of the wicked and bring them safely into the peace of his kingdom.

NOT A THING TO BE GRASPED. In this week's study we see Uzziah's pride: when Uzziah becomes strong, he uses his position to bring even more glory and honor to himself, putting himself in a position of utmost holiness and using God for his own glory. But how different is our God! Even though infinite glory belongs to him, according to Philippians 2:5–8 the Son of God did not consider such glory "something to be grasped." He did not take his honor as something to be hoarded, something to be shut away from the shameful things of this world. Rather, the Son of God humbled himself by taking human flesh to himself. In Christ, God in all his glory has come to dwell with lowly mortals, that we might enter into his glory.

Whole-Bible Connections

ANTICHRIST. Athaliah's determination to exterminate the Davidic line foreshadows Herod's attempt to wipe out the Messiah by massacring infants (Matthew 2). This is a manifestation of the wider strife between the serpent and the seed of the woman (Gen. 3:15), which appears in every attempt to use state-sanctioned violence to destroy God's faithful ones. Behind this violence is the great dragon, Satan, who pursues the woman about to give birth, in Revelation 12, and, after the Christ has been rescued, turns to persecuting the church. This might all be summed up as the spirit of antichrist: the attempt to destroy the Christ himself; and, failing that, to slaughter his followers. God's defeat of Athaliah's plans reflects the fact that the Antichrist is doomed to fall before the might of God.

THE ORDER OF MELCHIZEDEK. In the Old Testament, God establishes two separate institutions of kingship and priesthood, and it is important that they be kept separate. When a king such as Uzziah attempts to arrogate the office of priest to himself, idolatry is the result. The one exception to this pattern is Melchizedek, king of Salem and priest of God (Genesis 14). This is why Hebrews chapter 7 presents Melchizedek as a model of Jesus: because in Jesus, uniquely, the offices of both priest and king are fulfilled. Jesus, of course, never violates the sanctity of the Jerusalem temple or seeks to claim the office of priesthood at the earthly temple in Jerusalem. But, as the prophesied "priest forever after the order of Melchizedek" (Ps. 110:4; Heb. 7:17), Christ fulfills the ultimate realities to which the institutions of monarchy and priesthood pointed.

Theological Soundings

WISE COUNSEL. These passages highlight the importance of Christians seeking wise counsel. First and foremost, this means listening to the Word of God, ordering our whole lives under the authority of his revelation. But this also means ordering our lives and friendships so that we may have relationships in which we can seek wisdom. We must be willing to open our lives to the advice of others instead of acting only on our own wisdom. This includes attending to the preaching of God's Word and heeding our elders. Being good listeners, and listening to the right people, is an ethical imperative for those who are in Christ.

WORSHIP IN SPIRIT AND IN TRUTH. Sometimes we set rigid adherence to God's law against true, genuine, heartfelt piety. It is true that obedience can sometimes become legalistic. But the sin of Uzziah shows us that where our heart is, and what our liturgy looks like, are closely intertwined. Uzziah is not careful to follow God's law because he is proud, and so he seeks to have worship *his* way. But if we are humble and love God, this will result in a desire to follow his commandments carefully. True worship requires both a heart inclined to the Lord and careful attention to worshiping God in the way he has commanded.

Personal Implications

Take time to reflect on the implications of 2 Chronicles 21–27 for your own life today. Consider what you have learned that might lead you to praise God, repent of sin, and trust more deeply in his gracious promises. Write down your reflections under the three headings we have considered and on the passage as a whole.

1. Gospel Glimpses

2. Whole-Bible Connections

3. Theological Soundings

4. 2 Chronicles 21–27

> ### As You Finish This Unit . . .

Take a moment now to ask for the Lord's blessing and help as you continue in this study of 1–2 Chronicles. And take a moment also to look back through this unit of study, to reflect on some key things that the Lord may be teaching you.

WEEK 11: AHAZ
AND HEZEKIAH

2 Chronicles 28–32

▲

After the wise reign of Jotham, his son Ahaz leads Judah to new lows of idolatrous worship. However, after the low point of Ahaz, the Chronicler introduces us to Hezekiah, one of his best models of godly leadership. Hezekiah zealously restores worship in the temple, leads the nation in celebrating the Passover, and restores David's priestly organization. His firm faith is rewarded by the destruction of Sennacherib. The Chronicler holds Hezekiah up to his readers as an example of what returning to the pattern of David and Solomon should look like.

The Big Picture

The Chronicler contrasts Ahaz's tailspin into idolatry with the image of godly King Hezekiah, whose extreme zeal for the restoration of right worship leads to a prospering kingdom that need not fear even the mighty Assyrians.

Reflection and Discussion

Read through the complete passage for this study, 2 Chronicles 28–32. Then review the questions below concerning this section of 1–2 Chronicles and write your notes on them. (For further background, see the *ESV Study Bible*, pages 779–791; available online at www.esv.org.)

1. Ahaz (28:1–27)

In 28:1–4, whose example is Ahaz following, and whose example is he ignoring? According to the prophet Oded in verses 9–11, why does Israel defeat Judah? What does the response of the Israelites in verses 12–15 tell us about Israel? Is the northern kingdom irreversibly bad? How does this contribute to the Chronicler's portrayal of who "true Israel" is?

According to verses 16–24, where does Ahaz go looking for help? Can you think of any ways in which this might backfire?

2. Hezekiah's Reforms (29:1–31:21)

According to 29:3, when does Hezekiah begin the restoration of the temple? What does this tell us about his priorities?

Consider Hezekiah's speech in 29:5–11. According to Hezekiah, what is the cause of Judah's woes? Remember the story of Joash and the Levites' work on the temple. Why is it important that the Levites not be "negligent" (v. 11)? How do the Levites respond to the speech?

Consider 30:1–12. How do the inhabitants of the northern kingdom respond to Hezekiah's attempts to heal the divisions in the people of Israel? The scale of the Passover ceremony again tests the capacity of the temple staff (compare 29:34); how do they respond this time (30:15)?

The problem of uncleanness[1] recurs in 30:16–22. What does this episode say about the relative importance of cleanness according to the law, compared to the condition of one's heart?

Consider 31:2–10. Hezekiah sets out to restore the organization of the Levites instituted by David. What is Hezekiah's role in supporting and providing for the Levites? What is the people's role? What is God's role (v. 10)?

Why is it so important to the Chronicler that the king and the people support the Levites and give cheerfully from their own possessions? In verses 20–21, we learn that Hezekiah has obeyed God's law; what do these verses tell us about his attitude while obeying?

3. Sennacherib's Attack (32:1–33)

Consider 32:1–7. What steps does Hezekiah take to defend himself from the Assyrians? How do his efforts relate to faith in God? On whom is Hezekiah ultimately dependent (v. 8)?

Consider the Assyrians' theology as exemplified in verses 9–15. How do they think of their own strength relative to the gods of other nations and the God of Israel? On whom is the king of Assyria relying? What is the result (vv. 20–23)?

According to verse 25, what is the nature of Hezekiah's sin? In verse 26, how does Hezekiah respond to God's wrath? What is the result? How is Hezekiah an example of how believers struggle with sin? How is he an example of how we should respond when God brings suffering into our lives as a consequence of our sin?

___

What does verse 31 mean when it says that God "left him to himself"? How does this reveal Hezekiah's heart? Compare 2 Kings 20:12–19. Why would God allow sin into Hezekiah's life when this could have been avoided? What might be his purposes in testing Hezekiah?

___

Read through the following three sections on *Gospel Glimpses*, *Whole-Bible Connections*, and *Theological Soundings*. Then take time to consider the *Personal Implications* these sections may have for you.

▶ Gospel Glimpses

THE LAW IS FOR MAN. Although the Israelites sincerely desire to follow God, their uncleanness would usually have prevented them from participating in the Passover according to the letter of the law. But here we see God's compassion in pardoning this transgression so that the unclean can join with the people in worshiping him. This does not mean that carefully obeying the law is not important; rather, it exemplifies the principle that Jesus outlined when he said, "The Sabbath was made for man, not man for the Sabbath" (Mark 2:27). In other words, God's law is not meant to be a burden to oppress humans but is intended to liberate them by helping them live in the way that fulfills their God-given purpose. God's law is tempered by his mercy, because he knows our weakness.

SANCTIFIED IN CHRIST. The emphasis on consecration in this passage reiterates the importance of holiness in approaching God. In a sense, this sanctification is being accomplished in us now, as God's Spirit trains us in holiness and purges our sin. But there is also a sense in which our sanctification is a past event that has happened in Christ (Heb. 10:10). Christ has become for us sanctification (1 Cor. 1:30), which means that in Christ we have already been set apart and irreversibly consecrated to God's service. The call to obedience in the Christian life rests on this prior grace of God.

Whole-Bible Connections

ZEAL FOR THE HOUSE. Hezekiah exemplifies the zeal for God's temple that was already displayed by David and Solomon; he puts the right worship of God in the temple first, before everything else. Psalm 69:9 expresses this ideal quality of the Davidic ruler, one who can say, "Zeal for your house has consumed me." John 2:17 applies this statement to Jesus as he drives the moneychangers out of the temple. Jesus' zeal for his Father's house is expressed through a life of perfect worship and devotion to God, even to the point of death on a cross. It qualifies him as God's anointed king, through whom the world is called back to the true worship of God.

A ROYAL PRIESTHOOD. These passages highlight the importance of the priests and Levites consecrating themselves, and of all the people doing so as well. There is a sense in which all Israel was to be consecrated to God as a kingdom of priests (Ex. 19:6). In Christ, all believers are consecrated to God as priests; we are "a chosen race, a royal priesthood, a holy nation, a people for his own possession" (1 Pet. 2:9). Thus we become "living sacrifices" (Rom. 12:1) as our whole lives serve as acts of worship to our God.

Theological Soundings

REFORMATION. The reign of Hezekiah shows us the importance of reformation. Since sin always plagues us, the church often slips into periods of sin and decline. Thus the church is always in need of reform. But reform is not simply change for change's sake, or the updating of the church to reflect the latest cultural fads. Rather it is always a return to God's revelation in the past. The reform of the church must always be done according to Scripture: just as Hezekiah looked back to Moses and David in his reform, so we should look back to the Bible, seeking constantly to reform the church according to its teachings.

GOD'S DISCIPLINE. What does it mean when believers suffer? Scripture teaches us that God may use suffering in the lives of his saints to discipline them for their sin. Not all suffering is discipline for sin, and yet sin often does have negative consequences in our lives. This discipline does not mean that God is wrathful toward us, since there is for us no longer any condemnation (Rom. 8:1). In fact, God's discipline is an expression of the fact that he loves us as his children, and is disciplining us for our good. God may, by his mysterious providence, also allow us to fall into sin so that we might see the sinfulness of our hearts and our need of his grace and help. Though God may bring suffering into our lives, his final goal is always our good and his glory.

Personal Implications

Take time to reflect on the implications of 2 Chronicles 28–32 for your own life today. Consider what you have learned that might lead you to praise God, repent of sin, and trust more deeply in his gracious promises. Write down your reflections under the three headings we have considered and on the passage as a whole.

1. Gospel Glimpses

2. Whole-Bible Connections

3. Theological Soundings

4. 2 Chronicles 28–32

> ## As You Finish This Unit . . .

Take a moment now to ask for the Lord's blessing and help as you continue in this study of 1–2 Chronicles. And take a moment also to look back through this unit of study, to reflect on some key things that the Lord may be teaching you.

Definition

[1] **Unclean** – Lacking the status of ritual purity as defined by the purity laws of the Pentateuch. One could become unclean by not carefully observing these laws, e.g., by eating unclean animals, or through no fault of one's own, e.g., by contact with a dead body or by contracting a skin disease. It was important for those who entered the temple and participated in its rituals to be purified and thus in a state of ritual cleanliness.

Week 12: Manasseh, Josiah, and the End

2 Chronicles 33–36

After describing the high point of Hezekiah's faithfulness, the Chronicler relates Manasseh's descent into every imaginable kind of idolatry. However, the Chronicler also records Manasseh's exile, repentance, and restoration. Next, after recounting the sins of Amon, the Chronicler introduces the reader to Josiah, who carries out widespread and intense religious reform. However, at the end of his life Josiah fails to heed the Lord's word and subsequently dies at the hand of Pharaoh. The Chronicler then describes the last four kings of Judah in quick succession: all do evil in the eyes of the Lord, leading to their exile and to the destruction of the temple. However, the book ends on an optimistic note: God's discipline of exile is only for a set time, after which Cyrus decrees that the people of Israel shall return to their land.

The Big Picture

Manasseh's story proves that there is hope for repentance and restoration from exile even for the most sinful; Josiah shows us a model of how to walk in the ways of God; and the decree of Cyrus shows that, although God disciplines his people through exile, he remains faithful to his promise to dwell with them in the land.

> **Reflection and Discussion**

Read through the complete passage for this study, 2 Chronicles 33–36. Then review the questions below concerning this section of 1–2 Chronicles and write your notes on them. (For further background, see the *ESV Study Bible*, pages 791–798; available online at www.esv.org.)

1. Manasseh and Amon (33:1–25)

Consider 33:1–9. Manasseh's sins seem to be a laundry list of every conceivable idolatry. He is perhaps unique in the extent to which his idolatry penetrates into the temple itself (vv. 4, 7). How does verse 9 compare his sin to that of the Canaanites? How does Manasseh respond to God's warning, and what are the consequences (vv. 10–11)?

According to verses 12–13, why is Manasseh restored? Verse 13 says that Manasseh "knew that the LORD was God." What specifically does Manasseh learn about God from his experience? How might Manasseh's experience of deliverance from exile be an encouraging picture for the Chronicler's original audience?

What actions does Manasseh take when he returns from exile? Based on verse 17, how successful are these reforms?

Consider verses 21–25. In what ways is Amon like his father, and in what ways is he different? What does this tell us about the lasting consequences that sin can have, even if we repent?

----

2. Josiah (34:1–35:27)

Not only does Josiah walk in the ways of David, he does "not turn aside to the right hand or to the left" (34:2). This is the most ringing endorsement of any king since Solomon. In what ways are Josiah's actions in verse 3–7 more thorough than any of the previous reforms?

According to verse 9, from where do the funds come for the restoration of the temple? What does this tell us about the nation's involvement? According to verses 19–21, how does Josiah respond to hearing the Book of the Law? How does this contrast with other kings' responses?

According to the prophecy of verse 25, is there any hope of the exile's being forestalled? Why or why not? What do verses 26–28 say about why Josiah's fate will be different?

What do verses 29–33 say about the importance of God's Word and its place in the community of the people of God? What does verse 30 suggest about who needs to know the law, and how well they need to know it?

Neco's words in 35:20–21 are presented as the word of the Lord (perhaps surprisingly, given that he is an Egyptian pharaoh). How does Josiah respond? Notice that Josiah disguises himself before battle, ignores prophecy, and is shot by arrows in a chariot. Does this remind you of anyone (hint: see chapter 18)? What does this say about Josiah and the choices he makes here?

3. The Exile (36:1–23)

What do the last four kings of Israel have in common? What does verse 12 tell us about Zedekiah's heart? What does verse 13 tell us about why his rebellion against Nebuchadnezzar is especially sinful? What does verse 14 tell us about the involvement of the people in his sin?

What do verses 15–16 tell us about God? Is he hasty in his judgment? Does he enjoy smiting his people? Why is judgment necessary?

Consider God's judgment in verses 17–21. What is the significance of the destruction of the temple? Based on the theology of Solomon's prayer in 2 Chronicles 6, does the end of the temple mean that God's love is temporary or that he has forgotten his promises to Israel? What do verses 20–21 from our passage say about that possibility?

What does verse 22 tell us about who ultimately is sovereign over global politics? How would the words of verse 23 be encouraging to the people in the Chronicler's day? How would they be challenging?

Read through the following three sections on *Gospel Glimpses*, *Whole-Bible Connections*, and *Theological Soundings*. Then take time to consider the *Personal Implications* these sections may have for you.

Gospel Glimpses

HOPE FOR THE MOST SINFUL. Manasseh is an encouraging reminder that there is no one so sinful as to be completely beyond the reach of God's grace. In fact, God delights in bringing to himself those who are lost in their sin. Not only do we not need to be defined by the sins of past generations; we do not need to be defined by our own sinful past either. Anyone who turns to God in repentance will find God's compassion and love and will find himself to be part of a new story, a story of grace and redemption.

HIS STEADFAST LOVE ENDURES FOREVER. These last passages of 2 Chronicles truly drive home the invincible strength of God's promises. The intense sins of Manasseh cannot erase those promises, nor can the failures of even the best kings like Josiah. The hard-heartedness of God's people, persisting in sin and ignoring his calls to the point of exile and even the destruction of his temple, still does not lead God to totally reject his people. Rather, the exile has a prophetically defined limit (2 Chron. 36:21; compare Jer. 25:11–12), which will lead to the mercy of Cyrus and a new day, a new mercy of the Lord, and the chance to start over, dwelling with God in the land he gave to his people.

Whole-Bible Connections

THE PRODIGAL SON. A story like Manasseh's is reminiscent of Christ's own ministry. Jesus had a heart for particularly notorious sinners. As he points out in Mark 2:17, "Those who are well have no need of a physician, but those who are sick. I came not to call the righteous, but sinners." Jesus befriends gluttons, drunkards, tax collectors, prostitutes—all sorts of sinners. The outcasts of society find new hope of God's love through him. He shows the sort of love exemplified by the father of the Prodigal Son (Luke 15:11–32), which is so mystifying to the more obedient older brother. To the child who has insulted him and squandered all his money, he comes running in love, ready to forgive even before he is asked.

THE RETURN FROM EXILE. The decree of Cyrus quoted in the last verses of Chronicles is also quoted at the beginning of the book of Ezra (2 Chron. 36:22–23; Ezra 1:1–4). For the Chronicler, rest in the land is something that each generation must work for, and in keeping with that theme, return from exile to rest in the land is not something accomplished in an instant. Rather, it is something that must be fought for: Ezra and Nehemiah tell us about the obstacles facing the rebuilding of the temple and the walls of Jerusalem. There would be many opportunities to put into practice the Chronicler's call to participate in God's work and to throw in one's lot with God's people in obedience to the law and right worship. Each generation faces this challenge anew. In the Chronicler's day, even with a rebuilt temple, God's people still looked forward to God's restoration of a Davidic king, as he had promised. Ultimately, God's promises for restoration would not be fulfilled until the coming of his own Son, David's greater Lord, whose body is the true temple. And in a sense, we are still exiles (1 Pet. 2:11), awaiting the making new of all things promised to us in the return of Christ. Just as in the Chronicler's day, we are challenged to throw in our lot with God's king and to wait in patience for all of his promises to be fulfilled.

Theological Soundings

THE COMPASSION OF GOD. The picture of God's compassion for his people, shown in his repeated calls for them to hear and listen, reminds us that God's wrath should not be emphasized to the extent that we conceive of him as constantly irate, harsh, or vindictive. God takes no pleasure in the death of the wicked (Ezek. 33:11); rather, he is merciful, gracious, and slow to anger (Ex. 34:6). God is defined much more by compassion and love than by wrath. Nevertheless, God's wrath is a reality to be reckoned with. He will not tolerate sin or look the other way at injustice. God's justice and love are best displayed at the cross, which is an expression of both his wrath and his great love, as he takes the penalty of our sin upon himself to redeem us through the person of his Son.

GOD WITH US. The destruction of the first temple brought an important lesson for God's people. Later, Ezekiel would have a vision of God's glorious chariot on the banks of the River Chebar in Babylon, moving swiftly over the plains, far from the physical location of the temple (Ezekiel 1). The point is clear: God is not confined to the temple Solomon built. Though this was a painful reality for Israel to learn, there was a gracious dividend: God was able to be present with them even in exile in Babylon, without the temple. This is a lesson Jesus' disciples needed to learn as well. God came to dwell with his people in the body of Jesus Christ, but when it came time for him to ascend to heaven and be seated at his Father's right hand, he had to leave them. Jesus' physical body is now in heaven. But, in fact, it is to our advantage that Christ ascended on high, because he sent the Holy Spirit to us as our Helper (John 16:7). And so, by his Spirit, Christ promises us, "I am with you always" (Matt. 28:20). Although we do not see Christ presently, by virtue of his deity he is present with us, keeping us safe by his Spirit until the day when we all stand before our Father, worshiping in his heavenly sanctuary, where we shall see him face to face.

▶ Personal Implications

Take time to reflect on the implications of 2 Chronicles 33–36 for your own life today. Consider what you have learned that might lead you to praise God, repent of sin, and trust more deeply in his gracious promises. Write down your reflections under the three headings we have considered and on the passage as a whole.

1. Gospel Glimpses

2. Whole-Bible Connections

3. Theological Soundings

4. 2 Chronicles 33–36

▶ As You Finish Studying 1–2 Chronicles . . .

We rejoice with you as you finish studying the books of 1–2 Chronicles! May this study become part of your Christian walk of faith, day by day and week by week throughout all your life. Now we would greatly encourage you to study the Word of God on a week-by-week basis. To continue your study of the Bible, we would encourage you to consider other books in the *Knowing the Bible* series, and to visit www.knowingthebibleseries.org.

Lastly, take a moment to look back through this study. Review the notes that you have written, and the things that you have highlighted or underlined. Reflect again on the key themes that the Lord has been teaching you about himself and his Word. May these things become a treasure for you throughout your life— this we pray in the name of the Father and the Son and the Holy Spirit. Amen.

KNOWING THE BIBLE STUDY GUIDE SERIES

Experience the *Grace* of God in the *Word* of God, Book by Book

Series Volumes

- Genesis
- Exodus
- Leviticus
- Numbers
- Deuteronomy
- Joshua
- Judges
- Ruth and Esther
- 1–2 Samuel
- 1–2 Kings
- 1–2 Chronicles
- Ezra and Nehemiah
- Job
- Psalms
- Proverbs
- Ecclesiastes
- Song of Solomon

- Isaiah
- Jeremiah
- Lamentations, Habakkuk, and Zephaniah
- Ezekiel
- Daniel
- Hosea
- Joel, Amos, and Obadiah
- Jonah, Micah, and Nahum
- Haggai, Zechariah, and Malachi
- Matthew
- Mark
- Luke

- John
- Acts
- Romans
- 1 Corinthians
- 2 Corinthians
- Galatians
- Ephesians
- Philippians
- Colossians and Philemon
- 1–2 Thessalonians
- 1–2 Timothy and Titus
- Hebrews
- James
- 1–2 Peter and Jude
- 1–3 John
- Revelation

crossway.org/knowingthebible